CURRENCY CONV

This chart provides a table of prices converted from GB pounds, based on a conversion rate of $1.45 to the pound

£1	$1.45
£5	$7.25
£10	$14.50
£20	$29.00
£25	$36.25
£50	$72.50
£75	$108.75
£100	$145.00
£125	$181.25
£150	$217.50
£175	$253.75
£200	$290.00
£250	$362.50
£300	$435.00
£400	$580.00
£500	$725.00
£750	$1,087.50
£1,000	$1,450.00
£2,000	$2,900.00
£5,000	$7,250.00
£7,500	$10,875.00
£10,000	$14,500.00
£20,000	$29,000.00
£30,000	$43,500.00
£40,000	$58,000.00
£50,000	$72,500.00
£100,000	$145,000.00

ANTIQUES
UNDER £500

ANTIQUES UNDER £500

MARTIN MILLER

CONTENTS

£250–£500

ACKNOWLEDGEMENTS

GENERAL EDITOR
Martin Miller

EDITORS
Simon Blake
Marianne Blake
Abigail Zoe Martin
Peter Blake

EDITORIAL CO-ORDINATORS
Marianne Blake
Abigail Zoe Martin

PHOTOGRAPHIC/PRODUCTION
CO-ORDINATOR
Marianne Blake

PHOTOGRAPHERS
Abigail Zoe Martin
James Beam Van Etten
Anna Malni
Chris Smailes

How to Use This Book

by MARTIN MILLER

Due to the phenomenal success of my annual *Antiques Source Book*, we are now producing a series of specialist handbooks, each concentrating on a specific area of antique buying and collecting.

Antiques: Under £500 is a full-colour retail price guide to buying and collecting antiques on a budget. Divided into handy sections focussing on antiques and collectables costing under £100, those priced between £100 and £249 and those ranging from £250 to £500, it contains something to suit everyone's pocket.

The reason that this book stands out from other antique price guides is that we have used retailers, rather than auction houses, as our sources of information. Many of the items in this book are for sale at the time of going to press and a number, certainly some of the more arcane, will remain so for the lifespan of the book.

A reputable and experienced dealer's assessment of the price of an antique is at least as reliable – and usually a great deal more reasoned – than a price achieved at auction, and so even when the item you wish to purchase from the book turns out to have been sold, you have a reliable guide to the price you should pay when you happen upon another.

Should you spot something in this book that you wish to buy, simply note the dealer reference to the bottom right of the entry and look up the dealer's full name and details in the Directory of Dealers section at the back of the book. You can telephone, fax and, in many cases, visit the dealer's website.

All the dealers who have helped us with the book will be happy to assist you and, if the piece you wish to buy has already been sold, they will almost certainly be able to help you find another. Should you wish to sell an antique item, the relevant section and dealer reference will again be of help, but do not expect to be offered the same price at which the dealer is selling. We all have to make a living!

The price shown against an entry is per item, unless the heading and description refer only to more than one item, a set or a pair. Measurements are always given in the following order, as relevant: height or length; width or diameter; depth.

Good luck and good hunting!

Introduction

A new approach to antiques publishing, tailored to suit the buyer on a budget in a modern antiques marketplace.

The way that antiques are viewed and valued is constantly changing. The distinction between 'antique', 'collectable' and 'second-hand' has become very fuzzy in recent years.

Curiously, in this disposable age – or perhaps because so much is disposable – the artefacts of today are valued much more by modern collectors than their equivalents were by previous generations.

The definition of an antique has become more flexible, as technology has speeded up. This book takes a modern look at antiques by including such items as film posters, automobilia, kitchenalia, guitars, taxidermy, comic books and twentieth-century glass, ceramics, metalware, lighting and furniture.

Collectors who don't want to spend a fortune will be pleased to learn that modern antiques are not simply about monetary value. There are three other vital factors: quality, rarity and personal preference. If, like most of those collecting on a budget, you are doing it for the love of the subject, then trust your own judgement and, if you end up with something that may not be worth as much as you had hoped, at least you will enjoy owning it.

There are three traditional ways in which antiques change hands: at auction, in antiques fairs and markets and through retail dealers. In addition to these, there are direct sales through the placing of advertisements and, increasingly buying and selling directly on the Internet.

Antiques fairs and markets are great fun and a very painless way of buying cheaper antiques and hunting down some real bargains. These vary from the large, 'vetted' fairs, with serious dealers attending, to boot sales and charity fairs. Bear in mind that although everything tends to be fairly inexpensive, this doesn't necessarily indicate that it is a bargain – or that it is actually what it purports to be.

Permanent markets also provide an opportunity to pick up something of worth and collectable interest.

You can also visit our website on www.worldantiquesonline.com for a constantly updated treasure trove of antiques for gifts or for collecting, all at the right price!

Under £100

British Brooch ▼
- *2nd century AD*

Romano-British brooch. Lozenge-shaped with enamelled knob.
- £80
- Pars

Iron Statue ▼
- *circa 1950*

Iron statue of Ivan the Terrible in armour on horseback.
- *height 15cm*
- £50
- Zakheim

Turkish Vase ▲
- *circa 1930*

Twentieth-century Turkish, bottle-shaped vase with turquoise enamelling to body and neck and orange banding.
- *height 26cm*
- £90
- Sharif

Ivory Figure ▼
- *late 18th century*

Chinese carved ivory and bone figure of a young boy standing on a rock with a seal.
- *height 9cm*
- £80
- John Clay

Persian Beaker ◄
- *circa 1910*

Persian silver beaker with embossed foliate designs within shaped borders.
- *height 11.25cm*
- £50
- Sharif

Expert Tips

Prior to the 7th century, artists in Persia produced monumental figurative sculpture. After the Muslim conquests of the AD 600s, however, figurative sculpture almost ceased because Islam disapproves of making images of living things.

11

Architectural & Garden Furniture

Corbel ▲
- *circa 1840*
A terracotta corbel, used in the support of a projecting ledge, with acanthus-leaf and scrolled decoration to surface and architectural mouldings to sides.
- *height 40cm*
- £80   • Drummonds

Drain Hopper ▲
- *circa 1910*
Drain hopper with flower motif.
- *width 31cm*
- £35   • Curios

Garden Borders ▲
- *circa 1870*
Glazed terracotta garden borders with barley-twist top.
- *height 18cm*
- £6   • Curios

Pair of Folding Chairs ▼
- *early 19th century*
A pair of folding metal and wood green garden chairs.
- £80   • Old School

Chimney Pot ▼
- *19th century*
A glazed terracotta chimney pot. With banding and fluted design around the neck tapering to a square chamfered base.
- *125cm x 30cm*
- £80   • Old School

Terracotta Pot ▲
- *circa 1880*
A Victorian terracotta flower or garden pot of the classic shape, with drainage hole.
- *height 25cm*
- £15   • Curios

Paraffin Heater ▲
- *circa 1930*
A decorative paraffin heater, probably for use in a conservatory, with floral piercing to the top and base, a grilled door and coiled metal handle.
- *height 60cm*
- £45   • Curios

Arms & Armour

Brass Powder Flask ▼
- *circa 1840*

A larger than most brass powder flask, with brass nozzle for fowling or hunting.
- *length 25cm*
- £60   • C.F. Seidler

World War I Dagger ▼
- *World War I*

A World War I German fighting knife by "Ern". Has a studded wooden handle and is complete with a leather and steel sheath.
- *length 70cm*
- £70   • Chelsea (OMRS)

Lancer Chape Plate ▼
- *circa 1900*

Lancer chape plate with royal coat of arms and battle honours showing the Death Head of 17th Lancers.
- *height 12cm*
- £90   • C.F. Seidler

World War II RAF Cap ▶
- *1940*

A Royal Air Force warrant officer's uniform cap dating from the beginning of World War II.
- £85   • Chelsea (OMRS)

World War I "Brodie" Helmet ▲
- *1917*

A British army second type "Brodie" steel helmet, from the latter part of World War I, complete with adjustable leather strap.
- £75   • Chelsea (OMRS)

World War I German Helmet Badge ▲
- *1914*

The helmet badge of a Prussian soldier from the beginning of World War I, with the crowned eagle of the emperor and the inscription, "Mitt Gott für Koenig und Vaterland".
- *height 9cm*
- £50   • Chelsea (OMRS)

Boer War Two-Pound Shell Case ▼
- *1900*

A Boer War two-pound "Pom Pom" artillery shell case, in brass with projectile head in place but powder and percussion cap removed.
- *length 20cm*
- £15   • Chelsea (OMRS)

Great War Picture Frame ▼
- *1917*

A World War I picture frame made from the tip of a wooden aeroplane propellor blade, showing the photograph of a uniformed nurse from the period.
- £45   • Chelsea (OMRS)

13

Automobilia

Club Badge ▼
- *circa 1985*

Brighton Morgan Sports Car
Club. Perspex front on steel,
chrome-plated badge.
- £35 • CARS

Bugatti Book ▼
- *circa 1997*

Memoirs of a Bugatti Hunter by
Antoine Raffaëlli.
- *height 42cm*
- £32.50 • Motor

Bentley DC Badge ▲
- *circa 1960*

Bentley Drivers' Club badge in
pressed steel with alloy finish, in
green and white design.
- £45 • CARS

Morgan Badge ▲
- *circa 1990*

A "Morgan in Coburg" pressed
steel badge, with Art Deco
polychrome design, with front of
red Morgan in foreground.
- £30 • CARS

Club Badge ▼
- *circa 1958*

A radiator membership badge of
the Brighton & Hove Motor
Club, in navy-blue and sea-blue
chrome and enamel.
- £30 • CARS

Radiator Grill ▼
- *circa 1960*

A Mercedes radiator grill with
mascot and enamelled badge.
- *height 90cm*
- £50 • CARS

Formula I Book ◄
- *circa 1999*

A pop-up book entitled *The
Formula I Pack*, by Van der Meer.
- *height 32cm*
- £30 • Motor

Books, Maps & Writing Equipment

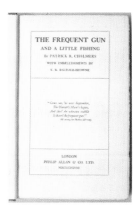

The Frequent Gun and a Little Fishing ▲
- *1950*
By Patrick R. Chalmers. Published by Phil Allan & Co., London
- *22.5cm x 15cm*
- £80 • Holland & Holland

The House of the Temple ▼
- *1930*
By Frederick W. Ryan. Burns Oates, London. A study of Malta and its knights in the French Revolution. First edition. 8vo. Numerous illustrations, original red cloth gilt. A very good copy.
- £95 • Bernard Shapero

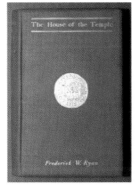

The Earth-Owl and Other Moon-People ▲
- *1963*
By Ted Hughes. Faber & Faber, London. First edition. Illustrated by R.A. Beard. Very good copy.
- *16cm x 23cm*
- £95 • Ash Books

Pencil Sharpener ▲
- *1930*
White plastic pencil sharpener showing a cricketer, made for the Australian Cricket team.
- *height 4cm*
- £55 • Jasmin Cameron

Travelling Inkwell ➤
- *circa 1860s*
Victorian travelling inkwell in original leather case.
- *height 6cm*
- £45 • Barham

Expert Tips

Centrally heated rooms are good for preserving books, as long as the atmosphere is not too dry.

Propelling Pencil ➤
- *1900s*
Ivory propelling pencil, decorated with painted enamel flowers, and silver mounts.
- *length 9cm*
- £79 • Langfords Marine

Ceramics

◄

Minton Trio
- *circa 1856*
Minton tea cup, coffee cup and saucer with Empire gilded design and pink bands.
- *height 7cm*
- £95
- London Antique G

Fabergé Cup and Saucer ▲
- *1894*
Fabergé cup and saucer with stylised leaf decoration to the saucer, the cup heavily gilded with lattice design on green base.
- *height 8cm*
- £85   • London Antique

Worcester Plate ▲
- *1811*
Worcester plate with hand-painted polychrome decoration.
- *diameter 22cm*
- £65   • A.D. Antiques

Fluted Cup and Saucer ▲
- *1890*
Meissen cup and saucer with fluted body, with floral decoration and gilding.
- *height 8.5cm*
- £88   • London Antique

Pepperette ▲
- *circa 1780*
A creamware pepperette, slightly damaged.
- *height 11cm*
- £75   • Garry Atkins

Davenport Trio ►
- *circa 1870–86*
Davenport ceramic trio of cup, saucer and plate, with Imari pattern.
- *diameter 16cm*
- *height 6cm*
- £75 each
- London Antique

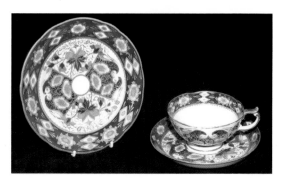

Dresden Tea Bowl ➤
- **1866**

Dresden tea bowl with two floral displays painted to the sides of the bowl by Adolph Hamann, raised on a circular foot and inscribed on the base "P223".
- *height 3.5cm*
- **£45** • London Antique

Soup Bowl ▲
- **1930–40**

A Susie Cooper soup bowl with a variegated pink glaze and a central pink rose.
- *diameter 23cm*
- **£85** • London Antique

Worcester Bowl ▼
- **1755–90**

A Worcester bowl of a fluted design with gilded floral decoration and a blue and gilded pattern around the rim.
- *height 18cm*
- **£80** • London Antique

Copeland Teapot ▲
- **1895**

Copeland teapot decorated with Burn's design incorporating chinoiserie scenes, with finial lid.
- *height 21cm*
- **£75** • A.D. Antiques

Shelly Jug ◄
- **1930**

A porcelain Shelly milk jug with swallow and pastoral scene with a yellow handle.
- *height 10cm*
- **£55** • London Antique

Splayed-Lip Jug ▲
- **1813**

Baker Bevin and Irvine jug of lobed design with splayed lip and transfer decoration.
- *height 15cm*
- **£95** • A.D. Antiques

Chamber Pot ◄
- **circa 1860**

A Victorian chamber pot, decorated with a floral design of roses, inscribed "Ridgways".
- *height 14cm*
- **£56** • Cekay

Delftware Tile ▼
- *circa 1720–60*
An English Delftware tile, London. The tile is slightly damaged. The design depicts an urn and floral arrangement.
- *height 14cm*
- £30
- Garry Atkins

Liverpool Tile ▼
- *circa 1760*
An English blue and white tile, made in Liverpool. The tile depicts a scene of a windmill within a diaper design.
- *height 14cm*
- £55
- Garry Atkins

Bristol Tile ▼
- *circa 1740–60*
Bristol tile depicting a European scene of an 18th-century lady in a pretty landscape.
- *height 14cm*
- £70
- Garry Atkins

Terracotta Tile ▲
- *1720–30*
English terracotta tile, with pattern showing musicians.
- *height 14cm*
- £95
- Jonathan Horne

Copper Goblet ▲
- *1840*
An English copper-lustre goblet, decorated with a floral design around the body with turned decoration.
- *height 12cm*
- £45
- Cekay

Royal Doulton Figurine ▼
- *1950*
A Royal Doulton ceramic figure of a young girl in a red and white dress and bonnet, holding a posy.
- *height 13cm*
- £95
- London Antique

Dresden Dancing Figure ▼
- *1945*
Dresden figurine depicting a Flamenco dancer, standing on an oval moulded base with gilding.
- *height 12cm*
- £65
- London Antique

Lustre Ware Mug ◄
- *1820*
A double-handled lustre ware mug, with floral decoration on a pedestal base.
- *height 12cm*
- £66
- Cekay

Clocks, Watches & Scientific Instruments

Russian Wall Clock ▼
- *1960*

An unusual geometrically designed Russian wall clock in painted red wood, with a white dial and a raised white circular hoop. Designed by Jantaz.
- *height 40cm*
- **£45**   • Radio Days

Cine Alpha Wrist Watch ▼
- *1940*

A gold-plated gentleman's Cine Alpha wrist watch, with black Arabic numerals on an orange band within a white dial.
- *diameter 3.5cm*
- **£95**   • The Swan

English Bakelite Clock ▲
- *1950*

An English brown bakelite clock with circular dial, free standing on square base and feet. Manufactured by Smith Electric of England.
- *15cm x 12cm*
- **£45**   • Radio Days

Military Issue Watch ▼
- *1940*

A military issue pocket watch by Waltman, with white Arabic numerals on a black dial with subsidiary seconds.
- *3.5cm diameter*
- **£75**   • The Swan

Dispenser's Scales ▼
- *circa 1930*

Scales in chromed steel on a mahogany base.
- *height 31cm*
- **£65** • Antiques Warehouse

Decorative Microscope ◄
- *Victorian*

A polished lacquered brass binocular microscope, which is purely decorative.
- *36cm x 15cm*
- **£79**   • Langfords Marine

Brass Rule ►
- *19th century*

Brass rule stamped "Arian", with multiple scales.
- *length 15cm*
- **£65** • Howard & Hamilton

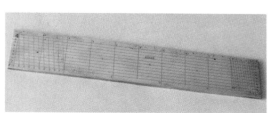

Coins & Medals

White Metal Medal ▼
- *d1852*

A white metal medal by Allen & Moore, commemorating the death of the Duke of Wellington.
- *diameter 50mm*
- £30 • Malcolm Bord

Soviet Military Medal ▼
- *1945*

World War II U.S.S.R. Order of the Red Banner Military medal awarded for valour to members of the Soviet army.
- £30 • Chelsea (OMRS)

Copper Medal ▲
- *1799*

A copper medal of William Pitt the Younger by Hancock, struck at a time when Pitt was enjoying great popularity due to victories over Napoleon in Egypt, notably the Battle of the Nile.
- *diameter 52mm*
- £40 • Malcolm Bord

Cap Badge ▲
- *1939–45*

Royal Armoured Corps WWII plastic cap badge.
- £25 • Chelsea (OMRS)

South African Medal ▼
- *1899–1902*

QSA (Queen's South African) Medal from the Boer War, with bars for OFS and Transvaal. Showing Queen Victoria and Britannia on reverse.
- £65 • Gordon's Medals

Imperial Iron Cross ▶
- *1914*

A World War I Imperial Iron Cross, Second Class with crown, 'W' mark, dated and with Friedrich Wilhelm crest.
- £20 • Gordon's Medals

Iron Cross ➤
• *1939*
A World War II German Iron Cross Second Class, awarded for bravery and / or leadership. Ring-stamped with swastika and with red and white ribbon.
• £38   • Gordon's Medals

India General Service Medal ⌄
• *1908*
India General Service medal with clasp, "North West Frontier". Awarded to 65 Barghir Daroska of the 51st Camel Corps.
• £60   • Chelsea (OMRS)

Iron Cross ▲
• *1914*
An Iron Cross Second Class, awarded to a German soldier at the beginning of World War I.
• £20   • Chelsea (OMRS)

General Service Medal ▲
• *1962*
A Northern Ireland service medal, awarded to L/CPL R. Scott, Scots Guards. With purple and green ribbon.
• £42   • Gordon's Medals

Military Medal Trio ◄
• *1918*
A trio of World War I medals, including the Victory medal, awarded to Private H. Codd of the East Yorkshire Regiment.
• £35   • Chelsea (OMRS)

Collectables

Pair of Hair Brushes ▼
- *1921*
A pair of tortoiseshell and silver
hair brushes with a silver
hallmark.
- *length 27cm*
- £55   • Aurum

French Lady's Compact ▲
- *1920*
A French Art Deco circular lady's
powder compact with a picture of
a young girl with auburn hair in a
romantic pose.
- *diameter 7cm*
- £65   • Linda Bee

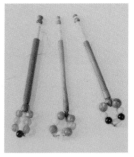

Talcum Powder ▼
- *circa 1950*
A "Jolly Baby" talcum powder
container, with voluptuous
cover.
- *height 15cm*
- £40   • Huxtable's

Thimble Case ▼
- *1760*
Ormolu thimble case with hinged
lid and embossed floral
decoration.
- *width 3cm*
- £98   • Thimble Society

Bobbins ◄
- *circa 1930*
Selection of three fruitwood
bobbins with beaded decoration
and carved stems.
- *length 19cm*
- £4 each   • Mathews

Gladstone Bag ➤
- *circa 1860*
Victorian crocodile-skin
Gladstone bag with leather
handle and brass fittings.
- *40cm x 26cm x 15cm*
- £70   • Henry Gregory

Coal Iron ▼
- *1880*

Dutch coal iron fitted with wooden handle.
- *height 22cm*
- £60   • R. Conquest

Mustard Tins ▼
- *1930s*

An assortment of Colman's mustard tins. Decorated with red writing and the Union Jack on a yellow background.
- *height 12cm*
- £7   • Huxtable's

Queen of Hearts Box ▲
- *circa 1920*

A sweet box from *Alice in Wonderland* in the shape of Tenniel's Queen of Hearts.
- *height 20cm*
- £75   • Huxtable's

Kitchen Scales ▲
- *1940s*

Set of British-made "Popular" kitchen scales in green enamel paint, with an accompanying set of brass weights.
- *height 45cm*
- £45   • Kitchen Bygones

Soda Siphon ▲
- *1960*

An English soda siphon with an emerald-green metallic plastic body and a black plastic lid.
- *height 30cm*
- £10   • Radio Days

Bottle Opener ◄
- *circa 1920*

A highly collectable Edwardian novelty bottle-opener in the shape of a lady's shoe, made of copper on cast iron.
- *length 12cm*
- £27   • Magpies

Pink Plastic Metallic Telephone ▲
- *circa 1965*
Pink plastic metallic telephone with black flex.
- *14cm x 14cm x 24cm*
- **£55**   • **Radio Days**

Genie Telephone ▼
- *circa 1978*
British Telecom special range, a much sought-after designer telephone in white with metal dial.
- **£39**   • **Telephone Lines Ltd**

Ericofon Telephone ▼
- *circa 1955*
Designed in 1953 by Ralph Lysell and Hugo Blomberg. In white and red with dial underneath.
- **£70**   • **Telephone Lines Ltd**

Star Trek Telephone ▼
- *circa 1994*
Modelled on Star Trek's "Enterprise" with sound effects and push-button dial to base.
- **£89**   • **Telephone Lines Ltd**

Brownie Box Camera ▼
- *circa 1960*
Brownie box camera flash model "B", with filters.
- **£30**
- **Mac's Cameras**

Polaroid Camera ▲
- *circa 1960*
The first Polaroid instant film camera – the 900 Electric Eye Land Camera.
- **£90**
- **Mac's Cameras**

Expert Tips

The important rule for the collector of "collectables" is to take care of the ephemera of today – they may be the antiques of tomorrow. The most collectable items are those that are in some way ground-breaking or revolutionary: for example, radios or telephones.

Gramophone Tins ➤
- *1910–50*
Assortment of gramophone
needle tins from around the
world.
- £15   • Huxtable's

Red Radio ▲
- *circa 1965*
A very Sixties round plastic red
portable radio, giving medium-
wave reception.
- £80   • Whitford Fine Art

Bakelite Radio ▲
- *1930*
Brown Bakelite radio with
lattice-effect front grille.
- £95   • Radio Days

Phonograph Cylinders ▲
- *circa 1900*
Three phonograph cylinders, two
from Edison and one from Bell, in
their original packaging.
- £25–45   • TalkMach

Knebworth Park ▼
- *5th July 1974*
Official programme for Pink
Floyd's open-air concert at
Knebworth Park, in performance
with other bands.
- £65   • Music & Video

The Verve ▼
- *circa 1992*
Mint condition copy of "Voyager
1", recorded live in New York by
The Verve.
- £65   • Music & Video

Tote Bag with Five 12-inch Singles ▲
- *1985*
Duran Duran tote bag containing
five maxi 12-inch singles.
- *30cm x 35cm*
- £75   • Music & Video

Pair of Beatles Stockings ▲
- *1960*
Pair of unused Beatles stockings
in original packet.
- *23cm x 17cm*
- £55   • Radio Days

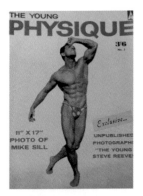

Young Physique ▲
- *1960s*

Issue no. 3 of the vintage muscle magazine *The Young Physique*.
- £4   • Book & Comic

True Romances ▼
- *November 1938*

November 1938 issue of women's magazine *True Romances*.
- £4   • Book & Comic

Playboy ▲
- *November 1968*

A 1968 issue of *Playboy* magazine with election cover.
- £8   • Radio Days

Viz ▲
- *1981*

Issue no. 7 of the adult humour comic *Viz*.
- £4   • Book & Comic

X-Men ▼
- *December 1977*

X-Men issue no. 108 – *Twilight of the Mutants* – published by Marvel Comics.
- £12   • Gosh

Rolling Stone ▲
- *1970*

October 1970 issue of US music magazine *Rolling Stone*.
- £6   • Book & Comic

The Atom ▶
- *1962*

First issue of *The Atom* comic, published by DC Comics.
- £40   • Book & Comic

Spawn ◀
- *May 1992*

Spawn magazine, issue no. 1, published by Image.
- £12.50   • Gosh

Egyptian Bank Note ◀
- *circa 1960*

Note of 10 pounds' value with a cartouche of King Tutankhamen. Uncirculated.
- £22   • C. Narbeth

American 15 Shilling Note ▾
- *circa 1773*

A colonial 15 shilling note, from Pennsylvania, with a prominent signature.
- £48   • C. Narbeth

Expert Tips

When collecting banknotes, always go for perfect condition and uncirculated notes if the issue is reasonably prolific. If the notes are rare, however, then the condition is not as critical.

Railroad Bond ▲
- 1866

Bond issued by the Boston Hartford Erie Railroad Co.
- £85   • C. Narbeth

French Revolution Note ▾
- *31st October 1793*

A five livre note dating from the French revolution. Extremely fine condition.
- £8.50   • C. Narbeth

Chinese Bond ▶
- 1913

Gold bond note issued by the Chinese Government.
- £25   • C. Narbeth

Decorative Arts

English Door Knobs ▼
- *circa 1890*
Pair of English beehive door knobs with brass mounts and turned decoration.
- *length 19cm*
- £85   • Myriad

Pair of Candlesticks ▲
- *circa 1930*
A pair of Art Deco chrome and decorative green plastic candlesticks with clear holders and conical sconces.
- *height 9cm*
- £42   • H. Hay

English Oil Lamps ▲
- *19th century*
Two English oil lamps in moulded light blue glass, with original fluted glass cover and polished brass respectively.
- *height 36cm*
- £70   • Old School

Pair of Candlesticks ▼
- *circa 1930*
A pair of chrome, two-branch candlesticks on circular bases, holding a sconce in each hand.
- *height 21cm*
- £78   • H. Hay

Table Lamp ▲
- *circa 1930*
Chrome and plastic table lamp with a glass shade.
- *height 41cm*
- £98   • H. Hay

Fruit-Shaped Lamp ▶
- *circa 1970s*
Italian plastic ceiling lamp in the shape of a peeled orange.
- *diameter 32.5cm*
- £60   • Zoom

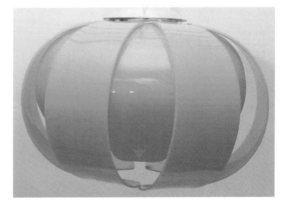

Furniture

Etched Sycamore Box ▲
- *circa 1900*

A sycamore box with etched scenes depicting the Isle of Wight.
- *6cm x 17cm*
- £55   • John Clay

Rice Bucket ▼
- *1880*

Chinese rice bucket with brass fittings, central carved handle and painted Chinese characters.
- *31cm x 25cm*
- £50   • Great Grooms

Sycamore Box ▲
- *circa 1900*

A small sycamore box with oval pictures depicting Western Road, Littlehampton.
- *8.5cm x 7cm*
- £34   • John Clay

Elm Stool ▲
- *circa 1710*

An early 18th-century English elm stool on four legs.
- *height 45cm*
- £95   • Castlegate

Painted Jardinière ▼
- *late 19th century*

Jardinière with painted steel body and floral scrolled handles.
- *height 21cm*
- £90   • Riverbank

Birdcage ▲
- *circa 1940*

A 20th-century birdcage of rectangular shape with covered back and sides.
- *height 31cm*
- £22   • Curios

Victorian Fire Screen ▲
- *1900s*

A brass fire screen with enamelled floral designs within a brass frame.
- *61cm x 43cm*
- £80   • Old School

Oak Stool ▲
- *1880*

A small oak stool, with solid seat, and standing on four rustically turned legs.
- *19cm x 31cm x 17cm*
- £85   • Lacquer Chest

Glass

Bristol Glasses ➤
- *circa 1885*
A cup, champagne beaker and
wine glass in blue glass.
- **£55 (for the 3)**
- Mousa

Mead Glass ▼
- *circa 1840*
A beaker-shaped green Bristol
mead glass.
- *height 11cm*
- **£75**   • Jasmin Cameron

Port Glass ▲
- *19th century*
A 19th-century port glass with
knop and domed base.
- *height 11cm*
- **£65**   • Jasmin Cameron

Pickle Preserve Jar ▲
- *circa 1825*
With an octagonal body, star base
and star stopper.
- *height 18cm*
- **£85**   • Jasmin Cameron

Babycham Glass ➤
- *circa 1960*
Babycham promotional
champagne glass.
- *height 12cm*
- **£14**   • After Noah

Coloured Wine Glass ◄
- *1890*
Cranberry-coloured wine glass
with long stem on a domed
foot.
- *height 11cm*
- **£65**   • Jasmin Cameron

Murano Glass Ashtray ◄
- **1950**

Fish-shaped Venetian Murano glass ashtray decorated with gold medallion splashes.
- 2cm x 8.5cm
- **£45**   ● Paolo Bonino

Biomorphic Bowl ▲
- **circa 1962**

A Holmegaard glass bowl by Per Lütken, with organic lines and a doubled, pinched lip.
- height 35cm
- **£90**   ● Circa

Stained Glass Panel ▼
- **circa 1910**

Decorative panel showing tulip-shaped floral image of nineteen geometric leaded sections.
- height 58cm
- **£45**   ● Curios

Czechoslovakian Scent Bottle ▲
- **1920**

An Art Deco smoky glass perfume bottle from the former Czechoslovakia, with a large pink silk tassel attached.
- height 12cm
- **£58**   ● Trio

Scent Bottle ▲
- **1901**

Small rose glass perfume bottle, diamond cut and faceted with clear stopper.
- height 3.5cm
- **£55**   ● Mousa

Expert Tips

The colouring in glass is achieved by using metallic oxides during the manufacturing process; white glass is obtained by using tin oxide during manufacture, while the famous Bristol blue is obtained by using cobalt oxide.

Monart Bowl ►
- **circa 1930**

A Scottish, aqua-green bowl, by Monart, with single-folded rim.
- height 8cm
- **£90**   ● Circa

Jewellery

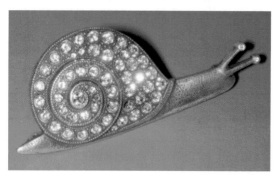

Snail Brooch ◀
- *1930*
A snail brooch in paste and silver.
- £65   • Linda Bee

French Brooch ▼
- *1950*
A French brooch styled as a pair of lady's legs with paste garters and red high-heeled shoes.
- *height 7cm*
- £85   • Linda Bee

French Ceramic Brooch ▲
- *1950*
A green French ceramic brooch in the shape of a poodle with bronze decoration and metal clasp.
- *length 5cm*
- £45   • Linda Bee

Green Lozenge-Shape Brooch ▼
- *1950*
Czechoslovakian brooch set with a dark-green lozenge stone surrounded by bright green, faceted stones.
- *diameter 5cm*
- £55   • Linda Bee

Fashion Ring ▲
- *1960*
Swedish ring with large central stone surrounded by metal band.
- £95   • Linda Bee

Fun Hooped Earrings ▼
- *1960*
English green plastic hooped earrings made in London.
- *diameter 4cm*
- £25   • Linda Bee

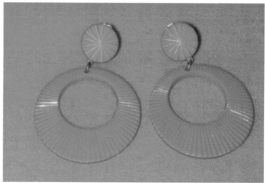

Headdress ◄
- *circa 1970*

Turkmen harem-style metal headdress with chain and plate pendant adornments and plated band with metal teardrop to centre with turquoise inset. Made in Afghanistan.
- **£83**
- Oriental

Mourning Brooch ◄
- *circa 1870*

A Victorian pinchbeck mourning brooch or scarf pin, with hair arrangement in the pattern of a flower, behind glass.
- *diameter 4.5cm*
- **£75**
- Sugar Antiques

Scarf Clip ▼
- *circa 1880*

Victorian brooch that can also be used as a scarf clip. Made of silver, with paste settings.
- *length 6cm*
- **£65**
- Sugar Antiques

Acrylic Rings ▲
- *circa 1965*

Moulded, clear acrylic rings with panels of colour running vertically throughout. Designed by Mary Quant.
- **£20**
- Themes & Variations

Marcasite Necklace ▲
- *circa 1950*

A marcasite necklace with bow and flower design.
- **£55**
- Sugar Antiques

Crystal Beads ▲
- *circa 1940*

A necklace of crystal glass, amber, faceted beads with the principal pendant an extremely large, cushion-cut stone in a pierced filigree mounting.
- **£35**
- Sugar Antiques

Brooch ▼
- *circa 1940*

Brooch of glass-encrusted flowers with blue beads.
length 7cm
- **£45**
- Sugar Antiques

Ethiopian Pendant ◄
- *circa 1890*

An Ethiopian silver pendant cross.
- *height 5cm*
- **£48**
- Iconastas

Marine Items

Parallel Rule ➤
- *circa 1800*

A 12-inch ebony parallel rule, for use in navigation. Unusual, with cut-out polished brass straps.
- £49   • Ocean Leisure

Anchor ▼
- *circa 1880*

Cast-iron ship's anchor.
- *height 1m*
- £80   • Curios

Telegraph ▲
- *circa 1880*

A brass model of the engine-room terminal of a ship's telegraph, with bone handle.
- *height 16cm*
- £90   • Sullivan

First Aid Kit ▼
- *1920s*

A rare and unique piece of shipping memorabilia, "First aid outfit for lifeboats", approved by the Ministry of Transport.
- *height 30cm*
- £99   • Langfords Marine

Prismatic Compass ▲
- *circa 1940*

An English brass, hand-held, military compass from World War II.
- £99   • Ocean Leisure

Magnifying Glass ▲
- *1837–1901*

Victorian magnifying glass with ivory handle and silver decoration.
- *length 19cm*
- £69   • Langfords Marine

Porthole ▲
- *1901–10*

Polished seven-inch diameter porthole made of brass with hinge and locking nut and six bevelled screw holes.
- *diameter 17cm*
- £69   • Ocean Leisure

Wooden Box ◄
- **20th century**

An oval wooden box with shipping scenes painted to the sides and the top showing a running battle between an English and a French man-of-war, both with all sails set and firing cannon on a turbulent sea.
- **£75** • Sullivan

Carved Coconut ▼
- **1880**

Victorian coconut with carving of a ship, cat, guitar, frog and foliage. These coconuts were usually carved by sailors.
- *length 6cm*
- **£85** • Langfords Marine

Luggage Labels ▲
- *circa 1930*

Cunard White Star luggage labels. Labels read "Not Wanted on Voyage", indicating that trunks should be stored in the hold, and "First Class", "Cabin Class" and "Tourist Class", in descending order of the social desirability of the owners.
- **£29** • Ocean Leisure

Ship's Linen ▲
- *circa 1950*

Souvenir linen from the Cunard company's RMS *Mauretania*.
- **£19** • Ocean Leisure

Scrimshaw Box ►
- *circa 1900*

A scrimshaw box with incised carving showing the central motif of a two-fluke anchor surrounded by breaking waves.
- *length 6cm*
- **£60** • Sullivan

Expert Tips

The best scrimshaw – the art of carving and inking whalebone or teeth, turtle-shell etc. – was produced by American whalers in the early 1800s. Scrimshaw was not only decorative. Sailors also produced useful things, such as needles, for their ladies.

Carved Tusk ◄
- **19th century**

A carved whale's tusk showing Caribbean scene, with compass mark. The initials "J.H. J.A." are on the reverse.
- *length 32cm*
- **£40** • Briggs

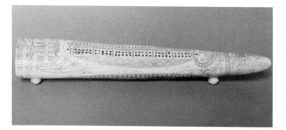

Silver & Pewter

Magnifying Glass ◄

Magnifying Glass
- *1813*
Silver magnifying glass with ornate handle and original lens. Birmingham.
- *length 19cm*
- £68   • Vivienne Carroll

Tobacco Box ▼
- *19th century*
A pewter oriental-style tobacco box with engraved floral designs.
- *height 8cm*
- £55   • Jane Stewart

Dutch Spoon ▼
- *circa 1900*
Water-carrier motif on engraved handle. Tavern scenes and pierced floral decoration.
- *length 23cm*
- £90   • Namdar

Pewter Spoon ▲
- *circa 1750*
Dutch pewter spoon, recovered from the River Thames with "Nature's Gilding".
- *length 15.5cm*
- £75   • Jane Stewart

Pewter Syringe ▲
- *1800*
A late Georgian pewter syringe.
- *length 19cm*
- £60   • Jane Stewart

Teapot ▼
- *circa 1850*
Pewter teapot, by Shaw & Fischer of Sheffield, with fluted spout and acanthus-leaf handle.
- *height 16cm*
- £65   • Jane Stewart

Victorian Cream Jug ▼
- *1860*
A Victorian pewter jug with scrolled handle.
- *height 7cm*
- £15   • Jane Stewart

Beaker ▼
- *circa 1785*

Swedish pewter beaker of fluted design with splayed foot.
- *height 14cm*
- £85   • Jane Stewart

Pewter Goblet ▲
- *19th century*

A pewter goblet with engraved decoration on a pedestal base.
- *height 18cm*
- £75   • Jane Stewart

Pilgrim's Badge ▼
- *15th century*

An early pewter pilgrim's badge.
- *height 5cm*
- £20   • Jane Stewart

Sauce Boat ▲
- *circa 1860*

Mid-Victorian sauce boat in Britannia metal (high-grade pewter), with pear-shaped body on three claw feet with scrolled, curved handle and moulded rim.
- *height 10cm*
- £50   • Jane Stewart

Half-Pint Tankard ▼
- *1840*

A half-pint tankard with scroll thumb piece and banding on a splayed base.
- *height 10cm*
- £45   • Jane Stewart

Early Georgian Tankard ▼
- *1740*

A pewter tankard of quart capacity with straight sides, banded waist and curved handle.
- *height 16cm*
- £85   • Jane Stewart

Set of Pewter Plates ▶
- *1750*

A set of four pewter plates with plain moulded borders, made in London.
- *diameter 15cm*
- £60   • Jane Stewart

Sporting Items

1920s Tennis Racquets ➤
- *circa 1920*

Tennis racquets with wooden handles and presses.
- £38 each
- Sean Arnold

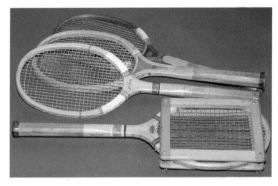

Shuttlecock Racquets ▲
- *1895*

Three Victorian shuttlecock and ping pong racquets, made of vellum with leather-bound handles.
- £5
- Sean Arnold

Cricket Bats ▼
- *circa 1920*

"Autographed" cricket bats – incised with names of famous players. Quality willow, English.
- £85
- Sean Arnold

Expert Tips

Golf has always been a sport for established, usually wealthy people and its artefacts collected. Golf clubs need to be in good condition, but can show signs of plenty of use.

Ice Axes ▲
- *1930*

Continental ice axes with wood handles and metal axe head, of various sizes. Hickory-shafted.
- *length 84cm*
- £60
- Sean Arnold

Hickory Golf Clubs ▲
- *circa 1910*

Hickory shafts. Leather grips and makers' names. Persimmon headed wood, hand-forged.
- £75, £45, £55, etc.
- Sean Arnold

Cigar Polo Mallets ➤
- *circa 1925*

Pair of cigar polo mallets with bamboo shafts, sycamore or ash heads. Made by Salters.
- *length 130cm*
- £48
- Sean Arnold

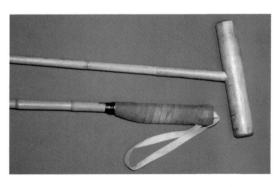

Football Medal ▼
- *circa 1920*
Silver enamelled football medal.
- £80 • Sean Arnold

Group of Handstitched Footballs ▲
- *circa 1920*
Group of 20th-century
handstitched leather footballs.
Made with 12 and 18 leather
panels. Best English cowhide.
With laces and bladders.
- £95 each • Sean Arnold

Hardy Fishing Lure ▼
- *circa 1940*
An unused "Jock Scott" lure,
manufactured by Hardy for
sea angling.
- £60 • The Reel Thing

Fishing Nets ▲
- *1900*
Fishing nets with bamboo shafts.
The net on the right is patent
collapsible.
- *length 78cm/left; 130cm/right*
- £90 • Sean Arnold

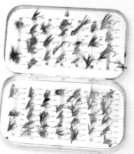

Football Rattle ▼
- *circa 1920*
Early 20th-century football rattle.
Made from wood and used by
football supporters. In good
condition.
- £75 • Sean Arnold

Bowling Balls ▼
- *circa 1910*
Lignum Vitae bowling balls with
bone monogram panels.
- *diameter 16cm*
- £60 • Henry Gregory

Three Fishing Reels ▼
- *circa 1900–30*
Selection of fishing reels. The
reels are made, from left to
right, of walnut and brass,
brass and steel.
- £45–65 • Sean Arnold

Fishing Flies ◄
- *1920*
Alloy cases containing trout and
salmon flies.
- *5cm x 9 cm/small
15cm x 9 cm/large*
- £90 • Sean Arnold

Tools

Brace ▼
• *circa 1830*
An ebony brace with steel chuck with the bit as a permanent feature, dating from the early 19th century, for use in the coopering trade.
• *length 40cm*
• £85   • The Old Tool Chest

Lady's Brace ▼
• *1860*
A beech lady's brace with cocobolo head.
• *length 27.5cm*
• £75   • Tool Shop Auctions

Mortise Chisel ▲
• *circa 1780*
A stonemason's mortise chisel for use in precision recessing.
• *length 33.5cm*
• £40   • The Old Tool Chest

Carved Router ▲
• *1780*
European fruitwood carved router with figured rosewood wedge.
• *width 15cm*
• £50   • Tool Shop Auctions

Watering Cans ▼
• *circa 1920s*
A selection of galvanised watering cans, one with an unusually large spout fitted in the top.
• from £24   • S. Brunswick

Set of Gardening Tools ▲
• *early 20th century*
A set of assorted garden tools, all with hornbeam shafts, including a 14-tine garden rake and a three-quarter spit trenching shovel. Mostly of steel construction.
• £48 each   • Myriad

Dado Plane ▼
• *circa 1780*
An 18th-century English dado plane, by the celebrated manufacturer John Green.
• *length 24cm*
• £24   • The Old Tool Chest

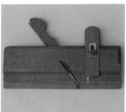

Garden Shears ▼
• *circa 1930*
A pair of tempered steel-bladed garden shears with turned ash handles. In working order.
• £25   • Curios

Plumb Bob ▼
• *1850*
Victorian steel-tipped brass plumb bob with brass reel.
• *length 8.8cm*
• £60   • Tool Shop Auctions

Toys, Games & Dolls

Barbie Doll ▲
- *1960*
Plastic flexible Barbie doll with
long blonde hair, a pink hairband
and pink pumps, by Matel.
- *height 30cm*
- £75   • Zoom

Merrythought Mohair Bear ▼
- *1930s*
Merrythought mohair bear.
A limited edition of 50 was
produced in white, brown and
black.
- *height 38cm*
- £55   • Dolly Land

Model Pandas ◄
- *1949*
Set 9011 in Britains Zoo series.
Giant panda standing on all fours
and two baby pandas (one on two
legs and the other on all fours).
With original box.
- £35   • Stephen Naegel

American Footballer ▲
- *1950*
American footballer with red and
white helmet.
- *height 9cm*
- £85   • Dr Colin B. Baddiel

German-Made Giraffe ▲
- *1950*
German elastoline Giraffe.
- *height 28cm*
- £75   • Stephen Naegel

Magic Roundabout ◄
- *1970*
"Magic Roundabout" characters,
on a red bicycle with a trailer,
made by Corgi Toys.
- *length 8cm*
- £45   • Dr Colin B. Baddiel

El des Colombus ▲
- *circa 1900*

Puzzle game, comprising several pieces that make up different shapes and instructions. Made in Germany.
- *10cm x 8cm*
- £80 • **Stephen Long**

Circus Elephant ▲
- *1950*

Clockwork grey circus elephant with blue eyes and red decorative trimmings.
- *height 14cm*
- £88 • **Dr Colin B. Baddiel**

Expert Tips

Many highly collectable toys are not particularly old, so it is worth visiting secondhand stores, junk shops, jumble sales and boot fairs to find the best bargains. Often, a very recent example of a popular toy is worth buying now for longterm value.

Wooden Garage ▶
- *circa 1950*

Wooden "Esso" garage with forecourt and petrol pumps. Original white paint with blue details. Includes hand-operated lift.
- *height 26cm*
- £85 • **After Noah**

Jigsaw ▼
- *1853*

Jigsaw of the Spithead Review 1853. Comprises key picture, taken from a contemporary painting, the original box and the complete jigsaw.
- *length 20cm*
- £37 • **Judith Lassalle**

Snap ▼
- *1920*

Pack of Snap cards, complete and in good condition with original box, depicting characters from the pantomime and nursery rhymes. British.
- £55 • **Judith Lassalle**

Tailless Donkey Game ▲
- *circa 1905*

"Pin the tail on the donkey" game, complete with donkey poster and tails and a curious snake.
- *49cm x 27cm*
- £55 • **Stephen Long**

Model Soldier ▲
- *1940*

First Empire Imperial Guard mounted standard bearer. Made in Belgium by M.I.M.
- *height 6cm*
- £80 • **Stephen Naegel**

Batmobile Car ◀
- *1960*

American black Batmobile, with red interior.
- *length 10cm*
- £48 • Dr Colin B. Baddiel

Rolls Royce ▲
- *1960*

Cream and silver Rolls Royce Phantom V made by Dinky.
- *length 8cm*
- £75 • Dr Colin B. Baddiel

Model T Ford Model ▼
- *1960s*

Dinky toy 109 cabriolet model of a Model T Ford car. Based on Gerry Anderson's TV series "The Secret Service". Black and yellow in colour. England.
- *length 8.5cm*
- £78 • Pete McAskie

Police Van ▲
- *1930s*

Black police van, made by Wells.
- *length 11cm*
- £75 • Dr Colin B. Baddiel

American Fastback ▲
- *1920*

American fastback orange car with black running boards and red enamel wheels, by Mano IL.
- *length 8cm*
- £75 • Dr Colin B. Baddiel

Fleischmann Train ▼
- *1955*

Fleischmann train with rails, in original box. HO-gauge.
- *width 38cm/box*
- £85 • Jeff Williams

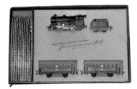

Miss Piggy ▲
- *1979*

Miss Piggy from the "Muppet Show" in pink sports car in famous waving pose.
- *length 11cm*
- £10 • Retro

Formula 1 Car ▲
- *circa 1950*

Lancia Formula 1 by Mercury of Italy. Unusual with petrol tanks on the side. With original box.
- *length 9cm*
- £78 • Pete McAskie

Union Pacific Train by Lionel & Co. ◀
- *1957*

Plastic orange Union Pacific train with black wheels by Lionel & Co.
- *length 28cm*
- £85 • Jeff Williams

Wine-Related Items

Oak Ice Bucket ▼
- *1880–1900*
Oak barrel ice bucket with silver plate banding and lid.
- *15cm x 13cm x 16cm*
- **£75** • Henry Gregory

Bottle Stopper ▲
- *early 20th century*
A silver-plated bottle stopper, probably continental.
- **£33** • Lesley Bragge

Double-Lever Corkscrew ▼
- *circa 1888*
An English Heeley double-lever corkscrew. Patent number 6606.
- *height 19.5cm*
- **£90** • Emerson

Handcup Decanter ▼
- *circa 1880*
A cylindrical Victorian lead crystal diamond-cut decanter.
- *height 32cm*
- **£95** • Barham

Liqueur Funnel ▲
- *circa 1820*
An early 19th-century fluted glass liqueur funnel of twisted shape.
- *height 13cm*
- **£55** • Jasmin Cameron

Barrel Tap ▼
- *circa 1890*
A steel barrel tap by Farrow & Jackson, with oval, open tap and square striking head.
- *height 16cm*
- **£50** • Emerson

Steel Corkscrews ➤
- *circa 1880*
Three steel corkscrews, two identical with folding handles and one with handgrip doubling as bottle opener.
- **£18–22 each** • Henry Gregory

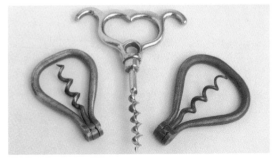

£100–£249

Babylonian Terracotta Statues ◄
- *1900–1750 BC*

A group of statues all relating to fertility, modelled in the form of female figures with emphasis on the breast.
- *average height 8cm*
- **£100 each** • Shiraz

Dagger ▼
- *circa 1000 BC*

A Persian, sand-cast bronze dagger from Luristan.
- *length 33cm*
- **£220** • Pars

Spearhead ▼
- *8th century BC*

Bronze, trowel-shaped spearhead, in fine condition. Persian from Luristan, Western Iran.
- *length 33cm*
- **£150** • Pars

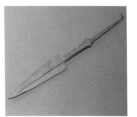

Clay Cylinder ▼
- *circa 2200 BC*

Royal cylinder bearing inscription of the King of Larsa.
- *length 33cm*
- **£220** • Pars

Face Mask ►
- *1st century AD*

A Romano-Egyptian face mask, with handle at back for holding in front of the face.
- *diameter 12cm*
- **£200** • Pars

Sri Lankan Figure ▲
- *circa 1800*

Female ivory figure from Sri Lanka, standing wearing pleated costume and necklace, with arms by her side.
- *10.7cm x 4cm*
- **£200** • Arthur Millner

Ink Holder ◀
- *circa 1870*

Persian ink holder decorated with bronze medallions along the shaft, from the Quarshar Dynasty.
- *height 25cm*
- £120 • Sharif

Roman Britain
'Piriform' variant
enamelled plate type
c 2nd.cent.AD

Found: Wiltshire

Persian Brass Dish ▲
- *circa 1910*

A Persian oval dish with engraved floral designs to centre.
- *width 40cm*
- £130 • Sharif

Russian Pendant ▼
- *18th century*

Russian bronze cross inlaid with turquoise and blue enamel.
- *3cm x 3cm*
- £220 • Iconastas

British Brooch ▲
- *2nd century AD*

Romano-British brooch. "Piriform" type, with pin, found in Wiltshire.
- £130 • Pars

Syrian Box ▶
- *1910*

Wooden box with mother-of-pearl inlay and red satin interior from Damascus.
- *25cm x 16.25cm*
- £120 • Sharif

Islamic Tray ▲
- *circa 1920*

Persian circular brass tray with engraved Islamic lettering and geometric patterns to centre.
- *diameter 58.75cm*
- £110 • Sharif

Wooden Toboggan ▶
- *1901*

Russian red-painted wooden toboggan from the Volodga region.
- *length 65cm*
- £120 • Zakheim

Architectural & Garden Furniture

Garden Lantern ▼
- *1920*

An oval wirework chinoiserie garden lantern, lined with decorative parchment on a circular wooden base.
- *height 60cm*
- £210   • Myriad

Garden Chair ▲
- *late 19th century*

A French metal garden chair, white-painted with pierced decoration to back and seat and scrolling to frame.
- *height 79cm*
- £210   • Myriad

Roofing Finial ▼
- *circa 1890*

Victorian terracotta roofing finial, with trademark "RCR".
- *height 18cm*
- £220   • Drummond

Stone Ball ◄
- *circa 1890*

A large, rough-hewn Yorkstone ball with good patina.
- *diameter 29cm*
- £200   • Curios

Expert Tips

When purchasing any terracotta objects make sure you look beyond the surface to see if there are any cracks beneath the grimy exterior. When buying second-hand roof tiles make sure you have seen the whole batch before you purchase, as often some of them may be cracked, damaged or discoloured. Town and country gardens are increasingly at risk from theft. Make sure that your garden antiques and statuary are properly insured and protected.

Pair of Stools ►
- *20th century*

A pair of rustic, twig-style garden stools in fruitwood.
- *height 47cm*
- £220   • Myriad

Arms & Armour

French Fireman's Helmet ▲
- *1895*
A highly ornate late-nineteenth-century brass French fireman's helmet, complete with red feather plume.
- **£225**   • Chelsea (OMRS)

English Civil War Piece ▲
- *1640*
English Civil War piece found in a castle moat. A linstock or Gunner's head. A touching off stick for firing cannon.
- *length 42cm*
- **£200**   • C.F. Seidler

British Navy Cutlass ▼
- *1899*
British Navy Cutlass without scabbard. Chequered leather grip. 1899 pattern dated April 1902 with sheet steel guard. Originally with leather scabbard and iron mounts.
- *length 85cm*
- **£130**   • C.F. Seidler

Regimental Belt Clasp ▼
- *1881*
Derbyshire Regiment special pattern officer's belt clasp; 95 per cent original finish. Blue enamel missing. Shown with Maltese Cross and recumbant stag within a wreath and oak leaf decoration.
- *length 10cm*
- **£175**   • C.F. Seidler

World War II Flying Helmet ▲
- *1944*
A World War II RAF "C" type flying helmet with intrinsic radio earpieces and MK VIII goggles with webbing strap and H-type oxygen mask for high altitude.
- **£185**   • Chelsea (OMRS)

German Sailor's Jacket ▲
- *1939*
A German naval rating's summer tunic from the beginning of World War II, with insignia.
- **£100**   • Chelsea (OMRS)

Islamic Stirrups ◄
- *17th century*
A pair of bronze Islamic stirrups finely engraved with floral designs.
- *height 15cm*
- **£150**   • Ghaznavid

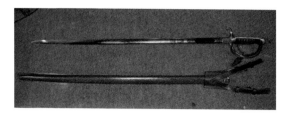

British Army Sword ◄
- *1920*

A post-World War I officer's dress sword belonging to an officer of the Royal Army Service Corps. The sword in steel with brass hilt and the scabbard in highly polished tan leather.
- *length 92cm*
- £185 • Chelsea (OMRS)

Boer War Chocolate Tin ▼
- *1900*

A hinged metal tin from the Boer War, originally containing chocolate and showing the royal crest, the profile of Queen Victoria, the inscription "South Africa 1900" and a signed message in the Queen's handwriting wishing the recipient, "A happy new year".
- *19cm x 11cm*
- £145 • Chelsea (OMRS)

Scottish Powder Flask ▼
- *circa 1800*

A Scottish powder flask, embossed with a shell pattern.
- *length 20cm*
- £180 • Holland & Holland

S.A. Dagger ▼
- *1933*

NSKK type with black enamel finish to scabbard. S.A. dagger etched blade with "Alles für Deutschland". Wood handle with Nazi insignia.
- *length 37cm*
- £245 • C.F. Seidler

American Trapdoor Trowel Bayonet ▼
- *1873*

American trapdoor Springfield trowel bayonet as used by plainsmen as a trenching tool and also as a defensive weapon.
- *length 36cm*
- £230 • C.F. Seidler

Lifeguard Boots ▲
- *1950s*

A pair of post-World War II dress boots of a trooper from the Royal Regiment of Lifeguards.
- *height 43cm*
- £150 • Chelsea (OMRS)

Cigarette Gift Tin ►
- *1914*

An example of a gift tin sent by Queen Mary to the troops fighting in France for the first Christmas of World War I. Complete with photographs, monogrammed cigarettes and all the original contents.
- *18cm x 11cm*
- £125 • Chelsea (OMRS)

Automobilia

Jaguar Mascot ▲
- *circa 1935*
An early version of the Jaguar
leaping-cat mascot, designed by
Gordon Crosby.
- £200 • CARS

Measuring Cans ▲
- *circa 1930*
Two-gallon and five-gallon
measuring vessels with copper
bodies and heavy-duty brass
banding. The cans show funnel
tops and brass spouts, positioned
to prevent over-filling. The five-
gallon vessel with hinged handle.
- £195; £180 • Castlegate

Expert Tips

*Collecting brochures of new
motor cars could be a wise
investment for the future.*

F3 Racing Pedal Car ➤
- *early 1970s*
A Tri-Ang plastic-bodied F3
racing car with dummy rear
engine.
- *122cm x 63cm*
- £150 • C.A.R.S

Motor Club Mascot ▲
- *circa 1915*
A Brighton & Hove Motor Club
dolphin in nickel-plated bronze
on a marble base. The oldest
motor club in England.
- £150 • CARS

RAC Badge ▼
- 1977
A Royal Automobile Club
Queen's Silver Jubilee badge –
a limited edition in chromium
plated and enamelled brass.
- £200 • CARS

Club Badge ▼
- *circa 1962*
A Brooklands Society badge in
pressed steel and chrome with
enamelling, showing an aerial
view of the track against a black
background. By Charles Sykes.
- £150 • CARS

Books, Maps & Writing Equipment

Gulliver's Travels ◀
- 1909

By Jonathan Swift. *Journey Into Several Remote Nations of the World.* Illustrated by Arthur Rackham. Published by J.M. Dent & Co., London. Fine quality.
- £150–180
- Adrian Harrington

East of Eden ▼
- 1952

By John Steinbeck. The Viking Press, New York. Superb copy in dustjacket. First edition.
- £120–150
- Adrian Harrington

The Loves of the Poets ▲
- 1860

Twelve steel plate engravings by the most eminent artists of the day. Published by W. Kent & Co (Late D. Bogue).
- *30cm x 23cm*
- £120   • Chelsea Gallery

Stiff Upper Lip, Jeeves ▲
- 1963

By P.G. Wodehouse. New York, Simon & Schuster. First edition preceded the London edition by five months. Very good quality.
- *14cm x 21cm*
- £100   • Ash Books

Tales of Mystery and Imagination ◀
- 1919

By Edgar Allan Poe. First edition. 4to. Original blindstamped limp suede. Rebacked preserving original covers.
- £150   • Bernard Shapero

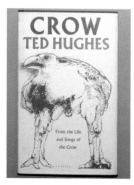

Crow ▲
- 1970

By Ted Hughes. From *The Life and Songs of Crow.* Published by Faber & Faber, London. First edition.
- *22cm x 15cm*
- £125   • Ash Books

Expert Tips

Wipe leather binding with a cloth smeared with Vaseline to help prevent it from drying out.

Aart Van America ▼

- *late 18th century*

Nieuwe K. Aart Van America. Published by D.M. Tangueld. Copper line engraving on paper with original hand colour. Dutch school.
- *22cm x 18cm*
- £195
- Ash Books

A Map of Portugal ▲

- *circa 1660*

Published by Johann Janssonius. Latin text. Figures taking scientific readings depicted in the heralding.
- *49cm x 38cm*
- £240
- Paul Orssich

Map of Vigo Harbour ▼

- *1750*

Map of the harbour of Vigo. Hills shown in profile and vegetation pictorially represented. Shows naval engagement in the Bay of Vigo, northwestern Spain.
- *47cm x 35.5cm*
- £120
- Paul Orssich

Print of Conil ▼

- *1580*

A print of the views of Conil. J. Gerez De la Frontera. The author is the publisher, Braun Hogenburg. Showing allegorical views of costume and trades of the 16th century.
- £220
- Paul Orssich

Map by J. Mettullus ▲

- *1601*

Very rare. Includes the Canary Islands. Showing galleons with slight lines and inset of Madeira.
- £220
- Paul Orssich

Spanish Sea Chart ▼

- *1799*

Published by the Spanish Hydrographic Office. Attributed to Vincent Tolfino of Cartagena. Fine copper engraving with minute detail and various depth readings. Good detail of the town.
- *52cm x 37cm*
- £140
- Paul Orssich

Glass Ink Stand ▼

- *circa 1925*

Art Nouveau green glass ink bottle resting on a brass stand.
- *height 8cm*
- £180
- Barham

Georgian Inkwells ➤

- *1810*

Late Georgian set of glass inkwells with lobed silver covers.
- *heights from 5cm*
- £180
- Jasmin Cameron

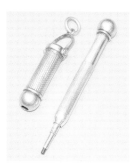

Telescopic Pencil ▲
- *1902*

Silver telescopic pencil in sheath with stirrup loop by Alfred Deeley, Birmingham, 1902.
- *length 3.75cm*
- £220 • Jasmin Cameron

Glass Ink Pot ▼
- *1870*

Victorian glass ink pot with faceted glass stopper and brass collar.
- *height 9cm*
- £135 • Jasmin Cameron

Brass Pen Rack ▲
- *1880*

Victorian six-tier brass pen rack on a square base with pierced foliate design.
- *height 13cm*
- £165 • Jasmin Cameron

Brass Letter Clip ▲
- *1843*

Victorian brass letter clip inscribed "Reg 3.10. 1843. Perry", by Pripson & Parker.
- *length 12cm*
- £175 • Jasmin Cameron

Novelty Pencil ▼
- *1870*

Victorian walnut and silver novelty pencil.
- *length 2cm*
- £225 • Jasmin Cameron

Pewter Ink Pot ▲
- *1850*

English Court House pewter ink pot inscribed "Stationery Office" on the base.
- *height 10cm*
- £155 • Jasmin Cameron

Marble Ruler ◄
- *19th century*

Polished black, pink, green, grey and yellow marble ruler.
- *length 25.5cm*
- £150 • Jasmin Cameron

Pencil and Paper Knife ►
- *1903*

Edwardian combination pencil and silver paper knife, made in Birmingham by Perry & Company.
- *length 15cm*
- £185 • Jasmin Cameron

Ceramics

Quatrolobe Set ➤
- *1890*

A Coalport Quatrolobe cup and saucer with pink and gold floral decoration.
- *height 2.5cm*
- £185   • London Antique

Sèvres Cup and Saucer ▲
- *1870*

Sèvres-style cup and saucer with gilding to the inside of the cup and the centre of the saucer, with gilt ribbons and swags on a dark cobalt-blue base.
- *height 5.5cm*
- £235   • London Antique

Royal Worcester Cup and Saucer ▲
- *1936*

An English Royal Worcester cup and saucer, with interlaced scroll decoration.
- *height 9cm*
- £150   • London Antique

Persian Bowl ▲
- *13th century*

A polychrome Persian bowl with a geometric design consisting of seven panels surrounding a central leaf pattern.
- *diameter 18cm*
- £100   • Pars

Art Nouveau Set ▲
- *1920*

Art Nouveau-style jug and bowl set, comprising five pieces.
- £195   • A.D. Antiques

A Soup Ladle ◀
- *circa 1780*

A creamware soup ladle with a scallop design. The item is slightly cracked.
- *height 29cm*
- £195   • Garry Atkins

Creamware Plate ▼
- *circa 1780–90*

A creamware plate, in excellent condition, with pierced rim.
- *diameter 24cm*
- £165   • Garry Atkins

Strawberry Plate ▼
- *1876*

Polychrome French Surrequenine strawberry plate with moulded strawberry decorations about the border, with gilding and jewelling on a light-blue base.
- *diameter 21cm*
- £245   • Jesse Davis

Minton Bowl ◄
- *1860*

Minton bowl with polychrome floral and gilt decoration, raised on a large footpad.
- *height 15cm*
- £225 • A.D. Antiques

Polychrome Tile ▲
- *1750–75*

A polychrome tile from Liverpool. The tile shows a floral design and some restoration.
- *height 14cm*
- £135 • Garry Atkins

Gouda Vase ◄
- *1926*

Zuid-Holland Gouda vase, of baluster form with flamboyant repeated organic pattern in blue, white and gold on a green ground. Made by C.A. Prins.
- *height 21.5cm*
- £225 • P. Oosthuizen

Floral Sugar Bowl ▼
- *1750*

Meissen sugar bowl with floral sprays to the cover and body.
- *height 8cm*
- £235 • London Antique

Satsuma Teapot ▲
- *1890*

Satsuma teapot, decorated with scholarly figures in a garden setting with rocks and foliage.
- *height 11cm*
- £155 • Japanese Gallery

Liverpool Tile ▲
- *circa 1770*

Liverpool tile, printed and overpainted in green enamel, showing an urn.
- £175 • Garry Atkins

Expert Tips

When purchasing Satsuma ware, the general rule of thumb is that the larger the item the better the price.

Wedgwood Plaque ◄
- *1768–80*

A Wedgwood cameo plaque dipped in black and white, showing four mischievous putti and mounted in a gilt frame.
- *20cm x 8cm*
- £200 • London Antique

Sweetmeat Dish ➤
- **1880**

Meissen sweetmeat dish showing a central figure between two scallop-shaped dishes.
- *17cm x 24cm*
- **£165**   • London Antique

Seated Shepherdess ◀
- *circa 1820*

A Staffordshire figure of a shepherdess seated on a flower-encrusted base with a goat.
- *height 135cm*
- **£135**   • Cekay

King Charles Spaniel ➤
- **1880**

A Victorian Staffordshire King Charles Spaniel painted white with green markings.
- *height 24cm*
- **£115**   • Cekay

Tea Canister ▼
- *circa 1800*

Tea canister showing rather comical scene of two ladies. Two gentlemen on reverse.
- *height 13cm*
- **£215**   • Jonathan Horne

Staffordshire Cottage ▲
- *circa 1860*

Staffordshire cottage with flower encrustation and triple bower front.
- *height 18cm*
- **£240**
- • Jacqueline Oosthuizen

Falstaff Toby Jug ▼
- **19th century**

A porcelain Toby jug of the Shakespearean character Falstaff.
- *height 24cm*
- **£225**   • Cekay

Clocks, Watches & Scientific Instruments

Silver Pocket Watch ▼
- *circa 1878*
English, large-sized silver chronograph, with key wind and key set. White-enamel face with black numerals and gold hands.
- **£195**　　　　• Sugar

Bulova Gold-Plated Wrist Watch ▼
- *1940*
A gold-plated gentleman's wrist watch by Mercheaz Bulova, with a white dial and gold baton numerals.
- *3.5cm square*
- **£150**　　　• The Swan

Fob Watch ▲
- *circa 1890*
A small, silver, Swiss fob watch with enamel dial and red numerals and gold floral pattern to centre, with incised floral decoration to covers.
- **£125**　　　　• Sugar

Small Silver Fob Watch ▼
- *circa 1890*
Silver hunter with enamelled dial with red numerals. Incised floral decoration to the cover.
- **£125**　　　　• Sugar

Gentleman's Incaflex Wrist Watch ▼
- *1950*
A gentleman's manual wind Incaflex wrist watch by Wyler with gold batons and Arabic numerals.
- *3.2cm x 2.8cm*
- **£140**　　　• The Swan

Pierre Cardin ◄
- *circa 1960*
Pierre Cardin-designed watch with original white-leather strap and Jaeger manual-movement.
- **£220** • **Themes & Variations**

Masonic Watch ◄
- *circa 1950*
A gold-plated watch with masonic symbols as numerals.
- **£150**　　　• A.M. P.M.

Pocket Barometer ◀
- *circa 1900*

A brass pocket aneroid barometer with silvered dial. The barometer is contained in its original hinged leather case. Compensated.
- *diameter 6.5cm*
- £160 • Howard & Hamilton

Military Marching Compass ▼
- *early 20th century*

A World War I hand-held prismatic military marching compass, in original anodised brass case. Government issue, denoted by the chevron.
- *6cm x 9cm*
- £169 • Langfords Marine

Dividers ▲
- *circa 1900*

A finely tooled pair of dividers by MDS Ltd London, in fitted leather- and velvet-lined box.
- *length 25cm*
- £200 • Howard & Hamilton

Microscope ◀
- *circa 1920*

A brass monocular microscope by C. Baker of London.
- *length 34cm*
- £130 • Howard & Hamilton

Nautical Protractor ▼
- *circa 1860*

Nautical protractor of 360°, with original velvet-lined mahogany box. By John Casarelli.
- *diameter 30cm*
- £150 • Talbot

Ship's Compass ▶
- *circa 1830*

All-brass ship's compass, on gimbals, with black and white dial, in a mahogany box.
- *length 12cm*
- £150 • Howard & Hamilton

Coins & Medals

Silver Penny ▼
- *circa 1025*
A short cross-type silver penny from the court of King Cnut.
- *diameter 32mm*
- £100 • Malcolm Bord

Crimean Medal ▼
- *1854*
Crimean Medal with Sebastapol bar. Officially impressed "E. Moss of the Coldstream Guards". With yellow and pale blue ribbon – Prince Albert's colours.
- £145 • Gordon's Medals

Gold Guinea Coin ▲
- *1794*
A gold George III guinea coin. This issue is known as the "Spadge Guinea".
- *diameter 19mm*
- £200 • Malcolm Bord

Breast Badge ▲
- *1933*
Knights Bachelor breast badge, silver gilt with red enamel background. From the Royal Mint with original box. Sword shown between two spurs.
- £220 • Gordon's Medals

Prize Medal ▼
- *1760*
Silver Wilhelmus de Wykeham medal from Winchester School.
- *diameter 33mm*
- £100 • Malcolm Bord

Military Badge ▼
- *1940*
WWII German navy U-boat badge, an early plated brass example.
- £225 • Chelsea (OMRS)

Medal Group ▼
- *1914–45*
WWI and WWII group of eight medals to Masters at Arms P. McArthur "H.M.S. Tamar".
- £225 • Chelsea (OMRS)

Collectables

American Handbag ▼
- *1950*

An American 1950s handbag with a handle of pink velvet, hand-painted with pink flowers.
- *16cm x 24cm*
- £150   • Linda Bee

Coca-Cola Card Sign ◄
- *circa 1940*

A Coca-Cola card sign with caption "Have a Coke".
- *height 65cm*
- £115   • Dodo

Disney Biscuit Tin ▲
- *circa 1939*

A Belgian biscuit tin showing various Disney characters.
- *length 30cm*
- £120   • Huxtable's

Austrian Art Nouveau Lady's Compact ►
- *1930*

An Austrian Art Nouveau lady's powder compact by Ledered in the shape of a suitcase with stickers.
- *length 8cm*
- £120   • Linda Bee

Michelin Ashtray ◄
- *1940s*

A premium give-away Bakelite ashtray with a seated figure in the form of the Michelin Man.
- *height 18cm*
- £150   • Decodence

Commemorative Tin ▲
- *1951*

A "Festival of Britain" commemorative tin.
- *6cm x 14cm*
- £200   • Huxtable's

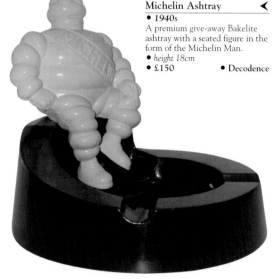

Chinese Snuff box ▲
- *1800–20*

Chinese tortoiseshell snuff box, deeply carved with figurative designs surrounded by a repetitive frieze.
- *length 8cm*
- £225   • Abacus Antiques

Small Sewing Machine ◄
- *circa 1900*
A "Stitchwell" hand-driven sewing machine.
- *height 14cm*
- £150 • TalkMach

Decorated Sewing Box ▲
- *circa 1840*
Rosewood sewing box decorated with mother of pearl.
- *width 30cm*
- £240 • Hygra

Needle Case ▼
- *circa 1890*
Ivory and mother-of-pearl needle case with hinged lid and silver cornucopia.
- *length 7.5cm*
- £149 • Fulton

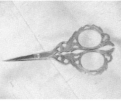

Italian Scissors ▲
- *circa 1770*
Steel eighteenth-century Italian scissors, with handles in the shape of peacocks.
- *length 13cm*
- £230 • Thimble Society

Black Telephone ▲
- *circa 1940*
Black bakelite telephone issued by G.P.O.
- £180 • After Noah

Edla Fan and Humidifier ▼
- *1930s*
A French Art Deco bakelite fan and humidifier,with a central circular metal cover.
- *height 35cm*
- £200 • Decodence

Mickey Mouse Telephone ▲
- *circa 1980*
British-made showing Mickey Mouse standing on faux-wooden base with push-button dial.
- £189 • Telephone Lines

Belgian Desk Telephone ▲
- *circa 1960*
A Belgian ivory desk telephone. Most of these were made in black, making this very collectable.
- £190 • Old Telephone Co

Minox Camera ◄
- *circa 1950s*

Minox A camera that was used in the World War II as a spy camera. It takes 8 x 11mm negatives, has a brushed aluminium body and a Complan 15mm, 3.5 lens.
- *1cm x 10cm*
- **£180**   • **Photo. Gallery**

Kodak "Girl Guide" Camera ▲
- *1933*

Blue Kodak "Girl Guide" camera with an F6.3 Anistigmat lens. Supplied with blue case.
- *13cm x 7cm*
- **£200**   • **Jessop Classic**

La Mort Aux Trousses/ North by Northwest ▲
- *1959*

Original French poster, paper backed, for the Hitchcock film *North by Northwest*.
- *79cm x 61cm*
- **£225**   • **Reel Poster Gallery**

16mm Cine Camera ▼
- *1928*

Bell and Howell 16mm cine camera with a 20mm F3.5 lens with 100ft spool, and a clockwork motor. The model is covered with grey tooled leather and is quite rare, especially outside the United States.
- *20.5cm x 3.7cm*
- **£150**   • **Jessop Classic**

Le Mans ▲
- *circa 1971*

French poster showing Steve McQueen. Artist Rene Fenacci.
- *61cm x 41cm*
- **£150**   • **Reel Poster Gallery**

Shirley Baker Print ▼
- *1964*

"Salford, 1964" by Shirley Baker. A silver gelatin print, signed verso.
- *30.5cm x 35.5cm*
- **£200**   • **Photo. Gallery**

Silver Gelatin Print ▲
- *1964*

"Martin Luther King at Oxford peace conference, 1964" by John "Hoppy" Hopkins. Signed verso.
- *25.5cm x 20cm*
- **£200**   • **Photo. Gallery**

JVC Television ▼
- *circa 1968*
A JVC "Space Helmet" television of spherical form on a square plinth. Monochrome reception.
- *height 60cm*
- **£200**　　● **TalkMach**

German Radio ▲
- *circa 1950*
A rare post-war German bakelite mains radio.
- *height 58cm*
- **£175**　　● **TalkMach**

Elvis 68 ▼
- *circa 1988*
A copy of the NBC TV *Comeback Special* commemorative Elvis Presley promotional album.
- **£125**　　● **Music & Video**

Set of Beatles Badges ▲
- *circa 1964*
With "I Love Paul", "I Love John", "I Love Ringo" & "I Love George". Tin badges with pin.
- **£195 (set)**
- ● **More Than Music**

Child's Gramophone ▼
- *circa 1940*
A German child's gramophone, in tinplate.
- *width 17cm*
- **£125**　　● **TalkMach**

Portable Gramophone ▼
- *circa 1920*
A Japanese portable gramophone, by Mikkephone, with unusual flattened horn speaker and carrying-case with strap.
- *width 30cm*
- **£200**　　● **TalkMach**

Kylie Promotional Handbag ▼
- *2000*
Promotional "Puma" handbag produced for Kylie Minogue's *Light Years* album. Contains full album and interview CDs.
- *20cm x 20cm*
- **£100**　　● **Music & Video**

Beatles Dolls ◄
- *1966*
Set of four NEMS/King Features syndicate inflatable cartoon dolls of the Beatles.
- *35cm x 15cm*
- **£120**　　● **Music & Video**

Decorative Arts

Chrome Syphon ▼
- *1960*

British-made chrome siphon and ice bucket.
- *height 40cm*
- £240　　　　　• **Zoom**

French Coat Hooks ▼
- *circa 1880*

A pair of French coat hooks in twisted brass with acanthus-leaf mounts and ceramic knobs.
- *length 16cm*
- £116　　　　　• **Myriad**

Bronze Prawn ➤
- *20th century*

A large model of a prawn in mother-of-pearl with verdigris bronze, in naturalistic pose.
- *length 27.5cm*
- £170　　　　　• **Butchoff**

Mexican Horse ▲
- *20th century*

A naively-modelled tin horse, with saddle and four straight legs, the whole on a square, tin base.
- *height 100cm*
- *length 120cm*
- £200　　　　　• **Curios**

Silverplate Bowl ▲
- *circa 1935*

Bowl with green bakelite base.
- *diameter 22.5cm*
- £175　　　　　• **Beverley**

Pair of Ball Candlesticks ▼
- *circa 1930*

Hollowed chromium-plated balls on a square base. American.
- *height 6.5cm*
- £120　　　　　• **Bizarre**

Statue of Boy ▼
- *1920*

A naturalistically carved sandstone statue of a boy seated on a rock.
- *height 60cm*
- £220　　　　　• **R. Conquest**

Iron Wall Lights ▲
- *circa 1930*

A pair of Italian painted iron wall lights with floral motifs.
- *height 36cm*
- £100 • **Rainbow**

Expert Tips

Make sure that cut-glass chandeliers and drops are intact, although in some cases they can be repaired with great success.

Anglepoise Lamp ▲
- *circa 1930*

Polished aluminium and chrome, designed by Cawardine, based on the constant tensioning principles of the human arm, and made by Terry & Sons.
- *height 92cm*
- £175 • **After Noah**

American Plaster Lamp ▼
- *circa 1950*

American plaster lamp with lady dancer for the base and a yellow lampshade with black tassels.
- *height 92cm*
- £175 • **Radio Days**

Oil Lamp Shade ▼
- *circa 1910*

Light blue opaque with waved, crimped edging. English, possibly Stourbridge.
- *height 21cm*
- £150 • **Barham**

Ceiling Star Light ➤
- *1900*

Moroccan star ceiling light of mirrored glass.
- *diameter 62cm*
- £240 • **Myriad**

Toile Chandelier ▲
- *1920*

French toile chandelier with painted flowers.
- *height 50cm*
- £200 • **R. Conquest**

Italian Chandelier ▲
- *1900*

Italian brass chandelier with splayed leaves and blue drop crystals.
- *width 45cm*
- £175 • **Rainbow**

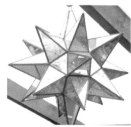

Furniture

Blanket Box ▼
- *1890s*
Nineteenth-century pine chest with scrolled apron, standing on bracket feet.
- *104cm x 49cm x 52cm*
- £220 • Old School

Tortoiseshell Box ▲
- *1930*
Atractive petite Art Deco tortoiseshell box.
- *length 10cm*
- £145 • Abacus Antiques

Tortoiseshell Box ▲
- *circa 1810*
Tortoiseshell cylindrical box with silver gilt trim.
- *height 12cm*
- £178 • Abacus Antiques

Occasional Chair ▼
- *circa 1890*
Louis XVI-style chair with caned seat and back.
- *height 90cm*
- £225 • Youlls

Bedroom Chair ▲
- *circa 1880*
A French gold bedroom chair with original upholstery.
- *height 90cm*
- £190 • Lacquer Chest

Country Armchair ▲
- *circa 1840*
An ash and elm country armchair showing good patination, with turned arm supports and legs.
- *height 91cm*
- £195 • Castlegate

Child's Rocking Chair ▶
- *circa 1900*
A turned child's rocking chair in ash and elm.
- *height 85cm*
- £145 • Castlegate

Bamboo Table ▼
- *early 20th century*
Bamboo and rattan table by
Maple in original condition.
- *height 66cm*
- **£240** • Christopher Howe

Bamboo Stand ▼
- *19th century*
A 19th-century bamboo stand
with tile inset.
- *height 82cm*
- **£170** • North West 8

Buffet Table ▲
- *circa 1830*
Mahogany two-tier buffet table in
original condition.
- *height 1m*
- **£240** • Christopher Howe

Bentwood Table ▲
- *19th century*
Round table with bentwood legs,
slightly splayed, and ball
decoration.
- *height 54cm*
- **£225** • North West 8

Edwardian Gong ▲
- *circa 1913*
An oak and horn gong with
baton and trophy plaque.
- *height 34cm*
- **£165** • Castlegate

Three-Tier Stand ▼
- *1890*
A three-tier mahogany cake
stand with fruitwood banding
- *height 89cm*
- **£195** • Great Grooms

Tile Table ▼
- *circa 1890*
Table of bamboo construction,
with legs and stretchers pale and
top darker, with inlaid tile to top.
- *height 47cm*
- **£120** • North West 8

Glass

Engraved Liqueur Glass ▼
- *circa 1880*
One of six, thumb-cut to bowl
with vine and fruit decoration.
- *height 9cm*
- £190 • Jasmin Cameron

Lemonade Jug ▼
- *1895*
Tankard-shape lemonade jug with
traces of gilding around the rim
and handle.
- *height 22.5cm*
- £185 • Jasmin Cameron

Monteith or Bonnet
Glasses ➤
- *circa 1750*
Mid-18th-century glasses.
- *height 8cm*
- £220 • Jasmin Cameron

Bristol Wine Glasses ▲
- *circa 1785*
A pair of tulip-shaped glasses
with a peacock-blue tint.
- *height 12cm*
- £235 (pair) • Jasmin Cameron

Georgian Rummer ▲
- *1810*
A Georgian rummer slightly
waisted bowl with unusual triple
banding, on a plain conical foot.
- *height 16.5cm*
- £110 • Jasmin Cameron

Port Glass ▼
- *circa 1810*
An early 19th-century port glass
with knops to stem.
- *height 10cm*
- £110 • Jasmin Cameron

Jelly Plate ▼
- *19th century*
Clear glass ice jelly plate, with
crenellated rims.
- *diameter 12cm*
- £130 • Jasmin Cameron

Victorian Decanter ▲
- 1890

Bohemian clear glass decanter with profuse gilded floral decoration, and faceted glass stopper.
- *height 32.5cm*
- £140 • Sharif

Pair of Blue Ewers ▲
- 1880

A pair of blue glass ewers with pinched lip and ribbon handle, enamelled with foliate designs.
- *height 24cm*
- £135 • Mousa

Scent Bottle ▲
- *circa 1880*

A Bohemian cut-glass scent bottle with stopper and floral gilding on a blue ground.
- *height 12cm*
- £210 • Mousa

Turkish Hooka ▲
- 1880

Turkish hooka used for smoking, the faceted and enamelled glass reservoir with brass apparatus.
- *height 123cm*
- £130 • Mousa

Cranberry Decanter ▲
- 1870

A Victorian cranberry-glass decanter with pinched lip, oversized clear glass stopper and moulded handle.
- *height 15cm*
- £165 • Barham Antiques

Scottish Gill Measure ▲
- 1810–50

Scottish measure of one gill, a quantity of spirit to be dispensed.
- *height 12cm*
- £240 • Jasmin Cameron

Georgian Finger Bowl ◄
- 1860–80

A mid-Georgian amethyst glass Stourbridge finger bowl.
- *height 9cm*
- £130 • Jasmin Cameron

Jewellery

French Art Deco Necklace ▲
- *1930*
A French green bakelite and silver link necklace.
- *diameter 2cm*
- £120　　　　● Linda Bee

Coro Duet ▲
- *circa 1940s*
Sterling silver coro duet brooch with removable fur clip, featuring green and black enamel stylised owls with green crystal eyes in paste settings.
- *height 5cm*
- £120　　　　● Hilary Conqy

American Metal Bracelet ▲
- *1940*
An American metal bracelet with bakelite plaques decorated with flowers.
- *height 2cm*
- £120　　　　● Linda Bee

Brooch ▼
- *circa 1965*
A "KJL" brooch, by Kenneth J. Lane. The brooch is of a flamboyant, baroque design, formed as a four-pointed star with rounded ends, set with a central, square cut faux cabochon ruby, and French lapis lazuli.
- *height 8cm*
- £150　　　　● Hilary Conqy

Zuni Ring ▼
- *circa 2000*
Zuni silver ring with a central sun symbol inset with jet and turquoise stones, surrounded by a feather design.
- *length 3.5cm*
- £169　　　　● Wilde Ones

Necklace and Bracelet ▶
- *1930*
German DRGM metal and paste necklace and bracelet.
- £195　　　　● Linda Bee

Navajo Ring ▲
- *circa 1940*
Turquoise and silver ring with stones set on circular plate. Turquoise has four globules of silver to each side.
- £199　　　　● Wilde Ones

Egyptian-Style Pendant ▲
- *1920*
An Egyptian-style hexagonal-shaped pendant with silver sphinx and teardrop amber stone.
- *length 2cm*
- £120　　　　● Linda Bee

Marine Items

Anchor Lamp ▼
- *circa 1940*

Copper and brass anchor lamp.
With "Seahorse" trade mark.
- *height 22cm*
- £180   • Ocean Leisure

Shipwright's Tools ▼
- *circa 1880*

Collection of four shipwright's
augers made of wood and iron.
- *68cm x 25cm*
- £180   • Langfords Marine

Bulkhead Clock ▲
- *circa 1920*

An eight day ship's bulkhead
clock marked "Smiths Empire",
with a painted enamelled dial
and Arabic numerals.
- *diameter 18cm*
- £240   • Langfords Marine

Expert Tips

*In the Napoleonic Wars
60,000 French prisoners of war
were billeted in England either
in prisons, or in prison ships,
and an industry sprang up to
help the prisoners buy personal
luxuries. The items made
by prisoners included model
ships, figures and chess sets,
and guillotines.*

Model Ship ▼
- *circa 1860*

A model of a four-masted clipper,
with long bowsprit, including all
rigging, deck fitments and figures.
Housed in a glass case.
- *height 42cm*
- £175   • Sullivan

Hand Bearing Compass ▼
- *circa 1930*

An ex-Royal Navy hand bearing
compass, gimballed and
contained in its original chest,
stamped "small landing compass
no.124/C".
- £189   • Ocean Leisure

Rolling Rule ◄
- *circa 1940*

Brass polished and lacquered
parallel rolling rule in original
box.
- *length 42cm*
- £149   • Langfords Marine

Silver & Pewter

Pewter Flagon ▼
- *19th century*

A pewter flagon and cover with a curving fish-tail thumb piece and C-scroll handle, made by Walker & Hall of Sheffield.
- *height 29cm*
- £120 • Jane Stewart

Bonbon Dish ▲
- *19th century*

Continental silver bonbon dish embossed with a central panel showing musicians in a wooded glade, with pierced surround.
- *length 13.5cm*
- £160 • John Clay

Cream Jug ▼
- *1802*

George III cream jug with ornate flower and scallop tooling and a ribbon handle.
- *height 12cm*
- £220 • Vivienne Carroll

Victorian Silver Goblet ▲
- *1896*

A fine silver goblet of conical form on a pedestal base made in Sheffield.
- *height 19cm*
- £225 • Stephen Kalms

Set of Pewter Goblets ▼
- *20th century*

A set of five, half-pint capacity, pewter goblets of typical form, in fine condition on a circular base. Handcrafted by Aquineas Locke of London.
- *height 15cm*
- £100 • Jane Stewart

Tudric Dish ▶
- *1895*

Art Nouveau by Liberty in polished pewter with hammered finish on a splayed pedestal foot, and organic, pierced handles.
- *diameter 32cm*
- £250 • Percy's

Sporting Items

Tennis Racquets ▼
- *circa 1900*
Three English lawn tennis racquets all with fishtail handles and convex wedges and thick gut stringing.
- *height 60cm*
- £245
- Sean Arnold

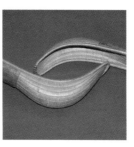

Hotspur Football Boots ▼
- *1920*
Pair of brown leather football boots with leather studs and cream laces, from a Hotspur footballer.
- *length 30cm*
- £225
- Sean Arnold

Ping Pong Bats ▲
- *circa 1880*
Pair of 19th-century ping pong bats. Head of bats made from vellum. Handles are tapered and made of mahogany. In good condition.
- *length 40cm*
- £125
- Sean Arnold

Wicker and Leather Pelota Cradles ▲
- *circa 1910*
Early 20th-century pelota cradles. Made from wicker with leather gloves. Used for high-speed ball game of Spanish origin.
- *length 50cm*
- £110 each
- Sean Arnold

Willow Cricket Bat ▼
- *1900*
Leather cricket bag with leather handle and straps, and willow cricket bat.
- *length 75cm*
- £120
- Sean Arnold

Signed Leather Football ▼
- *1950*
Mid 20th-century leather football recently signed by Vialli. The ball is constructed using twelve panels of handstitched leather.
- £120
- Sean Arnold

Leather Punchball ◄
- *1920*
Leather punchball with leather strap used to suspend it from the ceiling.
- *diameter 30cm*
- £185
- Sean Arnold

Starback Reel ▲
- *1910*

Starback wooden sea-fishing reel, with star-shaped brass mounts.
- *diameter 10cm*
- £115 • The Reel Thing

Milward Fishing Reel ▲
- *circa 1900*

Milward brass fishing reel with iron arm. Trade marked.
- *diameter 10cm*
- £245 • The Reel Thing

Landing Net ▲
- *circa 1930*

With bamboo handle and metal frame. Net intact.
- £125 • The Reel Thing

Boat Rod ➤
- *circa 1910*

Split-cane boat rod. 2m (7ft). Two sections.
- £125 • The Reel Thing

Wicker Creel ▼
- *1900*

Wicker-weave pot-bellied creel with sloping lid and fish slot, and webbing handle.
- *22cm x 22cm*
- £125 • Sean Arnold

Angler's Knife ▼
- *mid-20th century*

Unnamed angler's knife with six attachments including scissors in steel and brass. Sideplates marked with imperial scale 1–3 inches.
- £245 • The Reel Thing

Hardy Neroda Dry Fly Box ➤
- *circa 1920*

Hardy Neroda case with nickel-plated fittings, in tortoiseshell and bakelite. Compartmentalised into six sections with trout flies.
- £245 • The Reel Thing

Hardy Neroda Case ▲
- *circa 1925*

Large case with brass fittings and a metal liner with hooks to hang flies. Tortoiseshell and bakelite.
- £195 • The Reel Thing

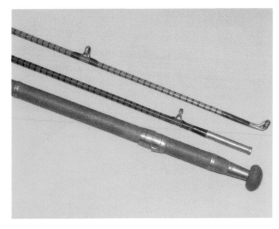

Tools

Rule and Measuring Stick ▼
- *1875*

Rare French Fisheries Officer's boxwood rule and iron measuring stick. The rule measures the denier of the nets to see if they comply with regulations. It has different scales on each face depending on the species being caught. The length of the fish is checked against the fish rule.
- *length 15cm*
- £200 • Tool Shop Auctions

Stanley 45E plane ▼
- *1923*

An immaculate Stanley 45E plane, a presentation piece in 1923. Type 15 Sweetheart, in a tin box, with instructions and original screwdriver.
- *length 25cm*
- £130 • Tool Shop Auctions

Rounding Plane ▲
- *circa 1850*

A rounding plane with original locking plates. Curved both ways, for use by a cooper or coach maker.
- *length 28cm*
- £130 • The Old Tool Chest

Brace ▲
- *circa 1780*

Late 18th-century brace, made by John Green, with brass chuck.
- *length 36cm*
- £140 • The Old Tool Chest

Trammels ▶
- *1870*

A rare set of four trammels with brass and steel tips, 17.5cm (7in).
- £140 • Tool Shop Auctions

French Watering Can ◀
- *circa 1930*

Enamelled French watering can of drum construction and screw-on lid, for indoor use.
- *height 38cm*
- £110 • Myriad

Victorian Plumb and Square ▲
- *1850*

A fine Victorian brass plumb and square with original patina.
- *length 27.5cm*
- £195 • Tool Shop Auctions

Garden Sprayer ▲
- *circa 1930*

Pressurised sprayer with copper and brass components, with copper cylinder and brass pump with turned wooden handle. Webbing carrying straps. All original materials.
- *height 77cm*
- £140 • S. Brunswick

Toys, Games & Dolls

Thunderbirds Doll ▼
- *circa 1966*

A "Brains" doll from the Gerry and Sylvia Anderson TV programme "Thunderbirds", complete plastic spectacles, spanner and pliers.
- *height 30cm*
- £200 • Dolly Land

Blue and Silver Metal Dalek ▼
- *1950s*

Unusual blue and silver metal dalek from the 1950s.
- *height 12cm*
- £225 • Dr Colin B. Baddiel

Celluloid Doll ▲
- *circa 1930*

A French celluloid doll in a green velvet suit and white blouse – both original. A "bent limb boy".
- *height 45cm*
- £145 • Dollyland

Pedigree Doll ▼
- *1950*

Pedigree doll in original dress. Walking doll with flirting eyes, naturalistic hair and red hair ribbon.
- *height 56cm*
- £110 • Big Baby Little Baby

Clockwork Circus Clown ◄
- *1930*

Clockwork Shiuko circus clown with a drum.
- *height 6cm*
- £145 • Dr Colin B. Baddiel

Snow White ▼
- *1938*

Snow White and the Seven Dwarfs, in painted lead. Part of Britains' Civilian Series.
- *height 4–6.5cm*
- £225 • Stephen Naegel

Magic Set ▲
- *circa 1860*

Two French painted tins with hidden compartments, for performing disappearing tricks.
- *height 13cm*
- £150 • Coleman

Expert Tips

Collectors of diecast models, such as Dinky Toys, demand that every mint model is accompanied by its original box.

Blue Mini ▼
- *1966*

Unusual blue Mini in original box, made by Dinky.
- *length 8cm*
- £125 • Dr Colin B. Baddiel

Hornby 4-4-4 Train ▼
- *circa 1920s*

Clockwork Hornby model of L.M.S. 4-4-4 locomotive, with original burgundy and black paint and brass fittings.
- *length 26.5cm*
- £195 • Wheels of Steel

Paper Puppet ▼
- *1870*

A German dancing paper puppet. A man holding a honey pot with tongue intermittantly protruding to lick it during dancing caper. Activated by drawstring.
- £195 • Judith Lassalle

Clockwork Whoopee Car ➤
- *circa 1930*

American clockwork tin plate orange Whoopee car. Grafitti on bonnet, for example "squeak easy". Makes crazy erratic movements. Illustrated on Maxime Pinksy vol. 2. Made by Louis Marx toys. Clown shown driving.
- *length 19cm*
- £245 • Pete McAskie

Bagatelle ▲
- *circa 1860*

German bagatelle board showing a sylvan scene on half-moon surface. Complete with original balls, six holes and in working order. With floral decoration.
- *height 46cm*
- £200 • Judith Lassalle

Hornby Pullman Coach ▲
- *circa 1930s*

Hornby series, "O" gauge Pullman coach with a beige roof and a dark-brown body. Windows with the original cellophane panes. Interior has lamps and curtains. Doors open and have keys.
- *length 33cm*
- £120 • Wheels of Steel

Wine-Related Items

Metal Corkscrew ➤
- *circa 1890*

Victorian metal corkscrew.
- *20cm x 9cm*
- £160
- Henry Gregory

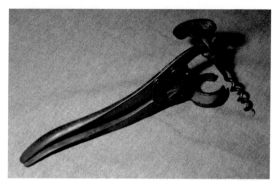

Clamp Wine Opener ▲
- *circa 1890*

Gaskell & Chambers clamp wine opener with extensive moulding.
- *height 24cm*
- £200
- Henry Gregory

Wine Bottle Pourer ▼
- *1880*

Silver wine bottle holder and pourer made by William Hutton & Sons of Sheffield, England.
- *height 24cm*
- £195
- Linden & Co.

Expanding Corkscrew ▲
- *circa 1902*

English expanding corkscrew by Armstrong.
- *27cm x 16cm*
- £120
- Henry Gregory

Decanter Label ▼
- *1809*

Thread design silver label with pierced letters "Sherry". By Phipps & Robinson, London.
- £140
- Linden & Co

Wooden Barman ▲
- *circa 1930*

An American syrocco wood barman with cocktail shaker.
- *height 20cm*
- £140
- Emerson

Punch Ladle ▲
- *1820*

Regency glass punch ladle.
- *length 22cm*
- £220
- Jasmin Cameron

£250–£500

Cuneiform Tablet ▼
- *2500 BC–1500 BC*

One of a group of Sumerian and Babylonian cuneiform tablets with administrative texts recording lists of produce, livestock and named persons.
- *length 10cm*
- £250 • Pars

Pilgrim's Flask ▼
- *1st millennium BC*

An Egyptian terracotta circular pilgrim's flask with spiral detail.
- *height 43cm*
- £250 • Pars

Egyptian Pot ▲
- *1st–3rd century AD*

Romano-Egyptian terracotta pot modelled in the shape of the face of Bes, the dwarf god.
- *height 6cm*
- *diameter 7cm*
- £400 • Pars

Camel Oil-Burner ▼
- *circa 2000 BC*

Stylized two-headed camel oil-burner with raised pillar on its back. Kerman, Southern Iran.
- *height 19cm*
- £400 • Shiraz

Ushabti ▲
- *1st millennium BC*

Egyptian blue-glazed *ushabti* with seven lines of hieroglyphic inscriptions, found in royal tomb.
- *height 17.5cm*
- £450 • Shiraz

Animal Figure ◄
- *9th–8th century BC*

Bronze model of a double-headed animal figure on four legs, with a head at each end. From Luristan.
- *height 6cm*
- £400 • Pars

Bust of Woman ▼
- *2nd century AD*

Terracotta bust of a Roman woman with good definition to hair, dress and face.
- *height 10cm*
- £300   • Shahdad

Brass Cross with Enamel Inlay ▼
- *circa 1830*

An unusually large brass Russian cross showing Christ on the crucifix, with enamel inlay.
- *41cm x 20.5cm*
- £390   • Iconastas

Quadratych ➤
- *circa 1840*

A brass and enamel folding quadratych depicting festivals and venerations of icons of the Virgin and Child.
- *17cm x 40cm*
- £290   • Iconastas

Ear Cup ▲
- *200BC–200AD*

A Han-dynasty ear cup of ovate shape and double handles with a green glaze. A tomb find.
- *height 11cm*
- £280   • J.A.N. Fine Art

Axe Head ▲
- *circa 8th century BC*

An axe head from Luristan, Western Iran, showing good patination.
- *length 18cm*
- £450   • Pars

Foundation Cone ▲
- *circa 2100 BC*

Foundation cone from Gudea, Sumarian for Ningirso warrior of Enil, ruler of Lagash.
- *length 14cm*
- £300   • Pars

Figure of a Female ▼
- *circa 1850*

Carved and painted alabaster figure in front of an orange shrine.
- *31cm x 14cm*
- £350   • Arthur Millner

Pottery Horse ▼
- *Tang Dynasty 618–907 AD*

Small red Chinese pottery horse decorated with black, yellow and white pigments, from the Tang Dynasty in the Henan Province.
- *20cm x 18cm*
- £450   • Little River

Architectural & Garden Furniture

French Chairs ▲
- *circa 1890*

A pair of metal chairs having curved seats with scrolled terminations and metal tassels and a heart-shaped back-splat.
- *height 61cm*
- £475
- R. Conquest

Stone Angel ▲
- *19th century*

Italian statue of a cherub embracing a pillar.
- £495
- Rainbow Antiques

Brass Sundial ▼
- *circa 1880*

A Victorian rustic sandstone sundial with a brass dial.
- *height 88cm*
- £285
- Tredantiques

Garden Recliner ▼
- *circa 1930*

A garden or conservatory recliner made from steamed and shaped bamboo with full-length cushion and original spoked wheels.
- *length 2.2m*
- £350
- S. Brunswick

Metal Arch ▲
- *circa 1870*

Decorative, wrought-iron, over-door arch of Gothic form with scrolled, foliate decoration inside and an outer arch with scrolled decoration within the border.
- *height 1.02m*
- £385
- Drummonds

Lion Mask ▲
- *1800*

An iron lion mask with terracotta patination.
- *diameter 35cm*
- £250
- R. Conquest

Arms & Armour

Army Officer's Home Service Helmet ▼

- *Edwardian*

A Royal West Kent Regiment officer's blue cloth home service helmet, with brass insignia and embellishments including spiked finial top.
- £450   • Chelsea (OMRS)

Dress Busby ▼

- *1916*

A dress busby with white plume and brass fittings and chin strap, showing insignia of the Royal Engineers and dating from World War I.
- *height 33cm*
- £275   • Chelsea (OMRS)

Indonesian Dagger ➤

- *19th century*

Indonesian *kris* dagger from Celebes with burr wood and gold and black lacquer. Silver mendak and nine lock pattern welded blade.
- *length 43cm*
- £280   • Robert Hales

Flintlock Pistol ▲

- *circa 1770*

30-bore flintlock box lock travelling pistol. Walnut slab butt.
- £400   • Ian Spencer

Rootes Colt ▲

- *1855*

.28-calibre Rootes colt. Five shot cap and ball revolver. Hexagonal barrel with a sheath trigger.
- *length 21cm*
- £495   • C.F. Seidler

Expert Tips

Rarity value aside, the most important quality to look for in a firearm is the "feel". Firearms must be well-balanced. Anything that feels top-heavy or unbalanced in the firing position loses value.

British SAS Uniform ▼

- *1990*

A British SAS sergeant's uniform and medals for the Falklands and Gulf War period (medals are replacements).
- £250   • Chelsea (OMRS)

Officer's Gorget ▼

- *circa 1830–1848*

Officer's gorget – Garde National de Paris. With original leather liner. Shield showing Bourbon cockerel over French flags with wreath choker.
- *height 14cm*
- £280   • C.F. Seidler

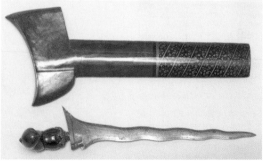

Automobilia

Wolseley Pedal Car ▲
- *late 1950s*

A Tri-Ang pressed-steel bodied model of a Wolseley with chrome detailing and working headlights.
- *105cm x 43cm*
- **£450**
- **CARS**

Ford Pedal Car ▲
- *early 1960s*

A Tri-Ang Ford Zephyr-style police car with working siren and chrome detailing.
- *84cm x 36cm*
- **£300**
- **CARS**

Japanese Cadillac ▲
- *1950*

A tin-plate Japanese 50s Marysan Cadillac, cream and green with working lights. Forward and reverse, very rare, in original box.
- *length 30cm*
- **£250**
- **Langfords Marine**

Expert Tips

The most famous car mascot, "The Spirit of Ecstasy", was created for Rolls Royce by Charles Sykes in 1910. The earliest mascot is the Vulcan Motor Company's, from 1903.

Badge/Trophy ▼
- *circa 1930*

A Brooklands Automobile Racing Club badge converted to a trophy, with enamelled decoration showing cars banking.
- **£450**
- **CARS**

Club Badge ▼
- *circa 1935*

A chrome and enamel member's badge for the Brighton and Hove Motor Club.
- **£300**
- **CARS**

Kneeling Spirit ▲
- *circa 1920–40*

A kneeling Spirit of Ecstasy, designed for the ergonomics of the bonnets of the Phantom III and the Silver Wraith.
- **£450**
- **CARS**

Jaguar Mascot ▲
- *circa 1936*

A Jaguar SS 100 leaping-cat mascot, mounted on a Panther J72 radiator cap.
- **£300**
- **CARS**

Bentley Mascot ▲
- *circa 1955*

The Bentley "Flying B" mascot, on the pressure cap of an "S" series Bentley.
- **£250**
- **CARS**

Books, Maps & Writing Equipment

A Grammar of Japanese Ornament and Design ▼
- *1880*

Japanese. By Thomas Cutler, with introductory text.
- *32cm x 38cm*
- £450   • Bernard Shapero

Through the Looking Glass ▼
- *1872*

By Lewis Carroll. Macmillan, London. First edition, 8vo. Illustrations by Tenniel throughout. Modern full red morocco gilt, all edges gilt.
- £350   • Bernard Shapero

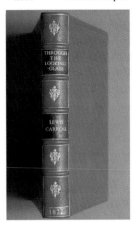

Bouquets et Frondaisana ▲
- *d1920*

By Segay Eugene. Original cloth backed portfolio. Paris. 20 sticky pochoir plates, comprising 60 designs based on flowers and foliage.
- *45cm x 32cm*
- £250   • Russell Rare Books

Bibliothèque des Predicateurs ▲
- *1716*

4 volumes. Full bound in 18th-century calf.
- £375   • Mark Ransom

The Old Curiosity Shop ▼
- *1841*

First edition of Dickens novel in good condition. Full calf binding and gilt floral decoration by Rowler.
- *height 16cm*
- £400   • Chelsea Gallery

The Sporting Adventures of Mr Popple ▶
- *1907*

By G.H. Jalland. Bodley Head, London. Landscape folio. Illustrated title page. Ten full-page captioned colour plates. each with facing illustrated textleaf in sepia. Original linen-backed colour pictorial boards. A very good copy.
- £250   • Bernard Shapero

English Map ➤
• 1680
By Robert Marden. Map showing the seasons in hemisphere. A prolific and inventive cartograph. Copper line engraving on paper. Hand-coloured.
• 15.5cm x 9.5cm
• £300 • Ash Books

Map of Africa ▲
• 1674
Map of Africa by Herbert Jaillot showing the Mediterranean and part of South Africa.
• £450 • Paul Orssich

Map by Ortelius ➤
• 1586
Ortelius was the first person to publish a map. Shows Iberian peninsula in full contemporary colour. The language text, page number and pagination signature are the key to dating the copper engraving on paper.
• 38cm x 50cm
• £250 • Paul Orssich

Synopsis Plagae Septemtrion alis Duecia Daniae ▲
• 1740
Copper line engraving on paper with original hand colour. Produced by the Augsberg geographer Matthaeus Seutter.
• 56cm x 49cm
• £450 • Ash Books

The Panorama. A Traveller's Instructive Guide ▲
• 1620
17th-century book, A Traveller's Instructive Guide. Published in London by J. Wallis & W.H. Reid. Original cover. 40 English county maps, 12 Welsh county maps. Clean and complete copy.
• 12cm x 9cm
• £250 • Russell Rare Books

Bertius of America ▼
• 1616
Engraving on paper. Originally produced for the 1616 edition of the Bertius Tabularem Geographicarum Contracterum libi Septem. Published by the younger Hadius at Amsterdam.
• 15cm x 11cm
• £350 • Ash Books

Chart of Mediterranean Sea ◄
• 1747
"A Correct Chart of the Mediterranean Sea" by Richard William Sene. Copper line engraving on laid paper. Originally produced for an English edition of Paul Rapin de Thoyzes (1661–1721). Translated by Nicholas Tindal (1687–1774).
• 71cm x 35cm
• £400 • Ash Books

Ink Blotter ◀
- *circa 1880*

English Victorian brass ink blotter with brass foliate decoration.
- *height 23cm*
- £485
- Barham

Mr Punch Paperweight ▼
- *19th century*

English silver-plated Mr Punch globe paperweight inscribed "The Punch always on top", by J. R. Gaunt.
- *height 12cm*
- £430
- Jasmin Cameron

Travelling Writing Box ▲
- *1850*

Wood and brass engraved travelling writing box. Includes inkwell, quill box, pen, pencil and rolling blotter.
- *13cm x 8cm*
- £485
- Jasmin Cameron

Waterman Pen ▲
- *1931–38*

Black and grey marbled Waterman Ideal fountain pen, No 32.
- *length 10cm*
- £270
- Jasmin Cameron

Letter Rack ▼
- *circa 1880*

Victorian pierced brass foliate designed letter rack, with a porcelain ink stand and a dark blue glass ink bottle, resting on a brass shield base with bracket feet.
- *25cm x 20cm*
- £295
- Barham

Vesta Box ▲
- *1820*

English bronze vesta box with greyhound on the top, from the late Edward and Alison Gibbons collection, Elm Hill, Worcestershire.
- *height 7cm*
- £320
- Jasmin Cameron

Parker Pen ▲
- *1942*

Parker Victory fountain pen in black and green laminated plastic.
- *length 12.5cm*
- £380
- Jasmin Cameron

Ceramics

Art Deco Coffee Set ◄
• *1930*
An Art Deco Carlton Ware
coffee set comprising six cups and
saucers, a sugar bowl, milk jug
and coffee pot. In emerald green
glaze with gilt banding and gilded
interiors.
• *height 27cm/pot*
• **£295**   • **London Antique**

Lobed Cup and Saucer ▲
• *19th century*
Meissen cup and saucer of lobed
decoration with scrolled handle
and painted panels.
• *height 6cm*
• **£395**   • **London Antique**

Chocolate Cup ▼
• *1890*
Dresden chocolate cup and saucer
with lobed rim and scrolled
double gilt handles. Decorated
with cartouches showing figures
in a garden setting within gilt and
jewelled borders, and floral
arrangements on a primrose
yellow ground.
• *height 7cm*
• **£285**   • **London Antique**

Swan-Handled Cup ▲
• *1860*
Sèvres-style cylindrical cup and
saucer, with a swan handle and
paw feet, and decorated with
floral sprays and gilding.
• *height 7cm*
• **£355**   • **London Antique**

Punch Bowl ▲
• *Qianlong period 1736–95*
Richly decorated in famille rose
enamels in the Mandarin style,
the exterior with two large panels
containing figures in a terraced
garden and two smaller
cartouches containing birds
perched on flowering branches.
• *height 8cm*
• **£275**   • **Anita Gray**

Kraakware Saucer Dish ▼
• *early 17th century*
Centre painted with an eight-
pointed star-shaped panel. With
moulded serrated rim.
• *diameter 14.5cm*
• **£380**   • **Anita Gray**

Cabinet Plate ▲
• *circa 1900*
A Vienna-style cabinet plate.
Hand painted, with a religious
scene of a martial angel aiding a
woman and children. Decorated
in gold with red scrolled panels
and green cartouches.
• *diameter 24cm*
• **£450**   • **Ian Spencer**

Expert Tips

*The colours of "famille rose"
were used on Chinese export
wares after 1720. The name
derives from the use of a
distinctive rose pink colour first
used in the reign of Qianlong.*

Kutani Jar and Cover ▼
- **19th century**
Kutani jar and cover, two panels with river setting. Dragon decoration on base and finial.
- *height 20cm*
- **£490** • **J.A.N. Fine Art**

Gouda Night Light ▲
- **1915**
Zuid-Holland factory. Design "A Jour". Made for La Marquise de Sevigne Rouzand'.
- *height 17.5cm*
- **£300** • **P. Oosthuizen**

Incense Burner ➤
- **1890**
Satsuma Koro incense burner decorated with gold figures.
- **£385** • **Japanese Gallery**

French Chinoiserie Vase ▼
- **1890**
French copy of a Chinese baluster vase with gilded chinoiserie designs on a blue ground.
- *height 48cm*
- **£425** • **Mousa Antiques**

Derby Vases ▼
- **1830**
A pair of small bottle-shaped Derby vases, gilded with flower encrustation.
- *height 11cm*
- **£285** • **London Antique**

Jug ▲
- **19th century**
A commemorative jug depicting the Duke of Wellington and General Hill in military fashion.
- *height 14cm*
- **£365** • **Jonathan Horne**

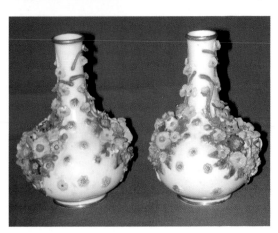

Cruet Set ▲

- 1865

A most unusual English or
Scottish cruet set consisting of
salt and pepper. The gentleman
is shown with a tri-cornered hat,
a red overcoat and a wry
expression.
- *height 91cm*
- £295   • Jesse Davis

Toby Jug ▲

- *mid-19th century*

A lady snuff-taker in green coat
with candy-striped underdress,
holding a snuff bag and taking a
pinch to her nose.
- *height 19cm*
- £260   • Constance Stobo

Pastille-Burner Cottage ▼

- *circa 1850*

Pastille-burner cottage with floral
design. Working chimney.
- *height 12cm*
- £295
- Jacqueline Oosthuizen

Terracotta Tile ▼

- *circa 14th century*

English terracotta tile with
grotesque design.
- *dimensions 11cm x 11cm*
- £435   • Jonathan Horne

Geometric Wall Tile ▼

- *13th century*

A polychrome Islamic wall tile
with repeating geometric pattern.
- *width 12cm*
- £290   • Ghaznavid

Spode Figure ▲

- 1910

A Spode figure of a lady in
courtly dress with chinoiserie
design, holding an extended fan
to her side.
- *height 12cm*
- £268   • London Antique

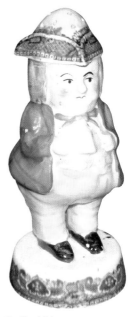

Staffordshire
Soldier Returning ▲

- *circa 1855*

Staffordshire "Soldier's Return"
depicting couple on a base
embracing after Crimean War.
- *height 21cm*
- £270 • Jacqueline Oosthuizen

Clocks, Watches & Scientific Instruments

"Moving Eye" Clock ◄
- 1930

Novelty dogs by Oswold, Germany. One eye is on the hour, the other on the minute.
- *height 14cm*
- £350
- Old Father Time Clock Centre

French Art Deco ▲
- 1939

Clock by JAZ. Typical of French Art Deco style. Maroon and black case with chromium embellishments. Embossed with stylised face.
- *height 18cm*
- £300
- Decodence

Smiths Mystery Clock ►
- 1930

English, 240v mains-powered, in chrome, bakelite and glass. Hands move without apparent reason.
- *height 22cm*
- £275
- Old Father Time Clock Centre

Art Nouveau Timepiece ▲
- *circa 1900*

French, polished brass. Cream white dial, faint pale blue arabic numerals and gilt hour markers. Eight-day French movement.
- *height 15.5cm*
- £450
- Gütlin Clocks

Gold Pocket Watch ►
- 1920

A gentleman's gold pocket watch with top-wind button set by Thomas Russell.
- *diameter 4cm*
- £250
- The Swan

Demi-Hunter Pocket Watch ►
- 1905

A 9ct. gold demi-hunter pocket watch by Wilson and Sharp of Edinburgh. With three-quarter plate movement.
- *diameter 4cm*
- £495
- Sugar

Lord Elgin Wrist Watch ▼
- *1950*

A rectangular, gold-plated Lord
Elgin gentleman's wrist watch
with subsidiary seconds by the
Elgin National Watch Company.
- *width 3.5cm*
- £275   • The Swan

Signed Rolex Watch ▼
- *1940*

A 9ct. gold lady's Rolex watch,
with a linked gold bracelet strap.
Back plate signed "MA".
- *2.5cm square*
- £275   • The Swan

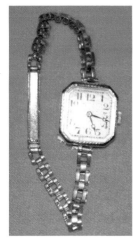

Asprey Rectangular ▲
- *circa 1916*

Silver Asprey rectangular curved
watch with white-metal dial and
Roman numerals.
- £260   • Sugar

Reading Glass ▲
- *circa 1760*

Glass with hand-painted horn
cover, floral arrangement to front
with putti and books on reverse.
- *length 12cm*
- £450   • Talbot

Horizontal Brass Sundial ▲
- *circa 1780*

Brass sundial with octagonal base
engraved with hororary table.
Gnomon with filigree decoration.
- *length 18cm*
- £380   • Talbot

Victorian Barometer ▼
- *1890*

A Victorian desk barometer with
silvered dial signed "Halstaf and
Hannaford, 228 Regent Street".
The setting hand is adjusted by
the ship's wheel.
- *height 32cm*
- £490   • The Clock Clinic

Dip Circle ▼
- *circa 1890*

All brass dip circle on tripod base
with screw-adjustable feet.
- *height 27cm*
- £380   • Howard & Hamilton

Three-Draw
Victorian Telescope ◄
- *1750–1817*

A three-draw Victorian telescope
signed "Dolland, London" on the
first draw. Polished and lacquered
brass with mahogany barrel, lens
slide, crisp optics.
- *73cm x 5cm*
- £329   • Langfords Marine

Coins & Medals

100-Franc Coin ▼
- *1904*
Gold Monaco 100-franc coin. Showing the head of Prince Albert I of Monaco.
- *diameter 34mm*
- £250 • Malcolm Bord

Austrian Coin ▲
- *1936*
Gold Austrian 100-schilling coin with Madonna on obverse and Austrian shield on reverse.
- *diameter 32mm*
- £450 • Malcolm Bord

Half-Sovereign Coin ▼
- *1817*
A gold King George III half-sovereign coin.
- *diameter 19mm*
- £250 • Malcolm Bord

Russian Order of St Stanislaus ▼
- *1900*
A Russian order of St Stanislaus, civil type 4th class. 18ct gold.
- £275 • Chelsea (OMRS)

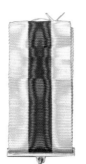

Military Cross ▲
- *1918*
In original case of issue and inscribed on reverse "2nd Lieut. S.G. Williams 1st Battalion, Devonshire Regiment".
- £325 • Gordon's Medals

Boer War Medal ▼
- *1893–1902*
A Boer War Queen's South Africa medal with seven clasps. Awarded to the 2688 Private G. Francis of the Welsh Regiment.
- £325 • Chelsea (OMRS)

Expert Tips

Bars on Victorian medals, indicating the actions within a campaign, add to the value.

WWI Medal Group ▶
- *WWI and later*
A WWI medal group of five medals, consisting of 1914–1915 Star Trio, 1935 Jubilee medal, RAF Long Service Good Conduct medal. Awarded to Corporal L. Thornton RAF.
- £250 • Chelsea (OMRS)

Collectables

White Friars ▲
- *circa 1880*
White Friars paperweight with concentric canes.
- *diameter 8.5cm*
- £290   • G.D. Coleman

St Louis Miniature ▲
- *circa 1855*
St Louis miniature paperweight with pink floral design.
- *diameter 4.5cm*
- £385   • G.D. Coleman

Lady's Pipe ▲
- *1880*
Small carved Meerschaum lady's pipe.
- *length 4cm*
- £350   • Langfords

Small Sewing Machine ▼
- *circa 1900*
An American "Little Comfort", handle-driven sewing machine.
- *height 17.5cm*
- £350   • TalkMach

Cloisonné Opium Pipe ▼
- *circa 1900*
Brass body with floral enamelling on a carved wooden base.
- £265   • Finchley

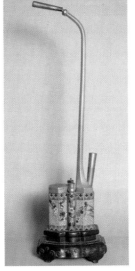

Mr Punch Cigarette Lighter ▶
- *circa 1920*
Silverplated with registered design mark on base. Lighter is underneath character's hat. Of English make.
- *height 16.5cm*
- £290   • Barham

Gold Thimbles ▲
- *1820–70*
Selection of continental gold thimbles, two with stone tops and one with foliate design, pearls and turquoise stones.
- *height 2.5cm*
- £325   • Thimble Society

Quiver-Shaped Case ▲
- *1730*
Mother-of-pearl needle case designed in the shape of a quiver.
- *length 9cm*
- £280   • Thimble Society

Travelling Case ➤
- *circa 1900*

English leather suitcase with
brass fittings and leather straps.
- *95cm x 56cm x 30cm*
- **£280**   • **Henry Gregory**

Victorian Hat Case ▲
- *circa 1870*

Victorian hat case in hide leather
with brass fittings and red quilted
interior. Designed to carry two
top hats and an opera hat.
- *height 87cm*
- *width 85cm*
- **£475**   • **Mia Cartwright**

Guinness Toucan ➤
- *1955*

A toucan with a glass of
Guinness on a stand advertising
the beer with the slogan –
"My goodness – my Guinness".
- *height 7cm*
- **£250**   • **Huxtable's**

Gladstone
Travelling Bag ▲
- *circa 1870*

All leather Gladstone bag with
brass attachments, two straps and
double handles.
- *length 69cm*
- **£480**   • **Henry Gregory**

Chrome handset ▲
- *1900*

A French candlestick telephone
with a metal base and chrome
handset by Thomson-Houston.
- *height 32cm*
- **£385**   • **Telephone Lines**

English Telephone ▼
- *circa 1900s*

An English telephone with a
wooden base, chrome bell and
metal handset by Electric and
Ordnance Accessories Ltd.
- *22.5cm x 20cm*
- **£295**   • **Telephone Lines**

Ivory Telephone ◄
- *circa 1930*

A GPO telephone in ivory, rare
for the period. Shows all-metal
rotary dial with original central
label and number / letter display.
- **£395**   • **H. Hay**

Midget Coronet Camera ▼
- *circa 1930s*

Art-Deco style, blue bakelite, Midget Coronet camera, fitted with a Taylor Hobson F10 lens. The colour is very rare.
- *2cm x 6cm*
- £325
- Jessop Classic

Half-Plate Camera ▼
- *circa 1900*

Sands and Hunter tail board 5x4 half-plate camera of mahogany and brass construction.
- £400
- Jessop Classic

Magic Lantern ▲
- *circa 1900*

Lancaster magic lantern used for projective hand-painted glass slides.
- £300
- Jessop Classic

Silver Gelatin Print ▲
- *1948*

"Movie cameraman in the South Pacific, 1948" by Cornel Lucas. Silver gelatin print, signed recto.
- *30.5cm x 40cm*
- £400   • Photo. Gallery

Audrey Hepburn ▼
- *1953*

Audrey Hepburn on Paramount Lot. Signed modern silver-gelatin print by Bob Willoughby.
- *length 30cm*
- £400
- Photo. Gallery

Silver Gelatin Print ▼
- *1965*

"March Climax, Trafalgar Square" London photograph by John "Hoppy" Hopkins.
- *length 40cm*
- £350
- Photo. Gallery

Signed Willoughby Print ◄
- *1962*

"Billie Holliday, Tiffany Club, 1962" by Bob Willoughby. A silver gelatin print, signed verso.
- *30.5cm x 35.5cm*
- £400   • Photo. Gallery

Phonograph ▲
- *circa 1900*
America Edison phonograph.
- *height 42cm*
- £250 • TalkMach

Portable Gramophone ▼
- *circa 1910*
English portable gramophone with lockable case and shaped arm with speaker attached.
- *width 34cm*
- £250 • TalkMach

Bush TV ▲
- *circa 1949*
Model 22 television produced by Bush. This was one of the most desired of all British Bakelite models.
- *height 39cm*
- £300 • Decodence

Diamonds Are Forever ▶
- *1971*
Original Japanese poster, paper-backed, style B.
- *76cm x 51cm*
- £350 • Reel Poster Gallery

Jungle Book Poster ◀
- *circa 1967*
Released by Buena Vista with credits to voice talents.
- *1m x 69cm*
- £300 • Reel Poster Gallery

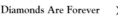

Star Wars Poster ▼
- *circa 1977*
With Polish translation and paper-backed. Artwork by Jakub Enol.
- *97cm x 69cm*
- £425 • Reel Poster Gallery

Official Brooch ▲
- *1964*
Official Nicki Byrne-designed Beatles brooch, with guitar and drum interwoven with the group's name and ceramic plaque showing their image, all on the original sales card.
- £250 • More Than Music

Sex Pistols Press Pack ▼
- *circa 1976*
"Glitterbest" press pack for *Anarchy in the UK* album. Twenty pages on white, pink and yellow stock, hand stamped.
- £482 • Music & Video

Decorative Arts

Coffee Pot and Cover ▲
- *circa 1880*
Coffee pot with engraved floral and geometric designs and enamel jewel inset.
- *height 34cm*
- £400 • Sinai

Brass Coffee Pot and Cover ▲
- *circa 1880*
A coffee pot from Bokhara, with elaborately swirled engraving and a pierced cover.
- *height 36cm*
- £400 • Sinai

Brass Water Jug ▼
- *circa 1890*
From Damascus with silver inset cursive Islamic script.
- *height 25cm*
- £450 • Sinai

Ecclesiastical Candelabrum ▼
- *circa 1900*
An ecclesiastical candelabrum of two sections, the upper half forming a triangular section with five candle-spikes.
- *height 165cm*
- £295 • Youlls Antiques

Islamic Dish ▲
- *circa 1890*
Brass, copper and silver dish with organic designs, the rim with Islamic cursive script.
- *diameter 26cm*
- £300 • Sinai

Copper Charger ▲
- *circa 1910*
Gilded, hand-crafted circular charger, exquisitely worked in a continuous band of flowerheads on a punched background.
- *height 30cm*
- £475 • David Pickup

French Candelabra ▲
- *1880*
A pair of French, decorative seven-branch metal candelabra.
- *height 65cm*
- £450 • R. Conquest

Oil Lamp ▲
- *19th century*

A Victorian oil lamp on a brass Corinthian column, with green glass reservoir vessel and all original fittings.
- *height 81cm*
- **£480** • Ranby Hall

American Batman Lamp ▲
- *circa 1940*

Polished steel adjustable lamp on a steel stand. Probably originally for medical use with heat-bulb. By Westinghouse.
- *height 106cm*
- **£275** • After Noah

Decorative Chandelier ➤
- *1920*

Toile chandelier with scrolling ormolu pink flowers and green foliage.
- *length 35cm*
- **£435** • R. Conquest

French Candelabra ▼
- *circa 1880*

French candelabra with cranberry-glass reservoir, three branches and chain link to gilded ceiling rose.
- *height 103cm*
- **£425** • R. Conquest

Hour-Glass Candelabra ▲
- *1920*

Italian candelabra with a metal hour-glass base and wire and green glass flower decoration.
- *60cm x 40cm*
- **£475** • Rainbow

Expert Tips

When considering large chandeliers or lanterns, take into account the weight and make sure the ceiling or wall fitting is durable enough and has been fitted correctly. Check whether the lamp or fixture uses a specialised bulb as part of its illumination, as some of these bulbs are unavailable in the shops today, and note the original wattage of the lamp.

Colomba Lamp ▲
- *1960*

Italian metal and glass, four globe, white Colomba lamp.
- *height 60cm*
- **£350** • Zoom

Furniture

Regency Tea Caddy ▼
- *1835*
Late Regency walnut-based
chevron-strung tea caddy with
two compartments.
- *12cm x 9cm x 13cm*
- £395   • J. & T. Stone

Reproduction Lowboy ➤
- *circa 1930*
Reproduction of a four-drawer,
eighteenth-century, walnut
lowboy, with crossbanded
marquetry and raised on cabriole
legs with pad feet.
- *height 75cm*
- £395   • Fulham

Merchant's Box ▲
- *18th century*
An Indian merchant's money box
with heavy iron hinges and
banding.
- *30cm x 38cm x 18cm*
- £260   • Gordon Reece

Butler's Tray ◄
- *circa 1810*
A mahogany butler's tray and
reading stand with turned and
tapered legs.
- *height 32cm*
- £480   • P.L. James

Kashmiri Box ▼
- *mid-19th century*
Polychrome painted papier
mâché octagonal box with
faceted sides decorated with
human figures, animals and
rambling floral designs.
- *10cm x 14cm*
- £350   • Arthur Millner

Hanging Shelves ▼
- *circa 1830*
Mahogany hanging shelves with
turned columns.
- *height 71cm*
- £475   • Lynda Franklin

Bow-Fronted Commode ◄
- *circa 1800*
A lift-top commode on splayed
feet with replacement mounts.
- *height 66cm*
- £420   • Albany

Gothic Stand ▼
- *late 19th century*

A stand of pentagonal form with gothic tracery.
- *height 110cm*
- **£450**   • **Youlls**

English Jardinière Stand ▼
- *circa 1870*

An English mahogany jardinière stand on a turned tripod base.
- *height 85cm x 34cm*
- **£390**   • **Tredantiques**

Art Nouveau Table ▲
- *circa 1918*

Art Nouveau table with organic inlay designs on four pierced legs.
- *height 81cm*
- **£420**   • **Castlegate**

French Basin Stand ▲
- *19th century*

A French mahogany basin stand with carved lyre-shaped supports.
- *height 77cm*
- **£495**   • **Rod Wilson**

Octagonal Rosewood Table ▼
- *1800*

An octagonal rosewood table with floral satinwood inlay, on tapering cabriole legs.
- *72cm x 78cm*
- **£450**   • **Tredantiques**

Cast-Iron Safe ▼
- *1880*

A solid cast-iron safe with four drawers at front and combination lock, marble-topped.
- *102cm x 54cm x 40cm*
- **£285**   • **Tredantiques**

Parisian Café Table ◄
- *circa 1920*

A small Parisian wrought-iron café table, on a heavy moulded cast-iron tripod base.
- *height 70cm*
- **£320**   • **Myriad**

French Giltwood Seat ▼
- *circa 1880*

Louis XV-style serpentine seat with four, carved cabriole legs.
- *height 44cm*
- £450   • Mark Constantini

Victorian Stool ▲
- *circa 1840*

Early Victorian carved stool in gilt with cabriole legs and salmon velvet upholstery.
- *height 18cm*
- £265   • Castlegate

Balloon-Back Armchair ▼
- *circa 1885*

With scrolled arms, on turned feet with original castors.
- *height 92cm*
- £395   • Castlegate

Mahogany Elbow Chair ▲
- *circa 1835*

With scrolled arm rests, turned front legs and sabre back legs.
- *height 81cm*
- £400   • Castlegate

Folding Campaign Chair ▼
- *circa 1870*

A folding campaign chair in green upholstery.
- *height 82cm*
- £330   • Lacquer Chest

Gothic Hall Chairs ▼
- *circa 1840*

A pair of Gothic chairs with period architectural back with the letters "A.S.".
- *height 92cm*
- £495   • Castlegate

Painted Fauteuils ◄
- *early 20th century*

A pair of French painted fauteuils in the manner of Louis XVI.
- *87cm x 60cm x 58cm*
- £350   • Westland & Co.

Glass

Pair of Victorian Goblets ◄
- *1880*

Extremely fine pair of matching Victorian goblets of super quality. The tall funnel bowls engraved with a fern pattern on barley twist stems by W. & J. Bailey E. Lerche.
- *height 20cm*
- £380 • Jasmin Cameron

Coin Glass Goblet ▲
- *1864*

Very rare coin glass goblet, with threepenny silver piece inserted in leg.
- *height 18cm*
- £400 • Jasmin Cameron

Georgian Rummer ▼
- *1809*

A late Georgian rummer, the notched bowl with terracing on a square flat foot.
- *height 14cm*
- £340 • Jasmin Cameron

Blue Bohemian Goblet ▲
- *1880*

Blue Bohemian glass goblet with a waisted bowl on a pedestal foot with white foliate design and gilt banding.
- *height 18cm*
- £340 • Mousa

Toddy Lifter ▲
- *1825*

Exceedingly rare toddy lifter from the early nineteenth century.
- *height 18cm*
- £350 • Jasmin Cameron

Pair of Lithayalin Beakers ◄
- *1880*

A pair of white Bohemian Lithayalin beakers, of waisted form in translucent glass, the outer surface cut with broad facets, with gilding.
- *height 12cm*
- £380 • Mousa

Art Deco Scent Bottles ◀
- *1920*
A pair of English Art Deco
perfume bottles in clear glass
with black geometric designs.
- *height 18cm*
- £268   • Trio

Bohemian Vases ▼
- *circa 1895*
A pair of green overlay vases with
strong geometric patterns.
- *height 27cm*
- £480   • Mousa

Venetian Vase ▲
- *19th century*
Mille fiore double-handled vase
in perfect condition.
- £400
- Shahdad

French Bottle ▲
- *circa 1850*
A French bottle and stopper with
applied brass decoration and lid,
with ornate handles.
- *height 21cm*
- £370   • Mousa

Cameo Scent Bottle ▼
- *circa 1860*
An English cameo scent bottle
engraved with flowers and leaves.
- *height 8cm*
- £260   • Mousa

René Lalique Ash Tray ▲
- *1920*
Cendrier ashtray incorporating
a celtic design on the border,
signed "Gao' René Lalique".
- *diameter 9cm*
- £450   • Jasmin Cameron

Mercury Bottle ▲
- *1880*
A very rare perfume bottle in cut
red glass with a moulded silver
hinged stopper.
- £310   • Trio

Jewellery

Cornelian Brooch ▼
- *1890*

Arts and Crafts silver brooch of a foliate design set with cornelians, by Amy Sonheim.
- *diameter 4cm*
- **£280** • **Gooday Gallery**

Christian Dior Brooch ▼
- *1960*

Circus horse brooch by Christian Dior.
- **£295** • **Linda Bee**

Turquoise Beads ▲
- *circa 1930*

Antique spider web turquoise beads, from New Mexico, which have been restrung with new clasp on a silver chain.
- *length 60cm*
- **£499** • **Wilde Ones**

Fob Seals ▲
- *1840*

Two 18ct gold English fob seals, ornately decorated with pineapples and foliage. With carved agate stones.
- *height 3.5cm*
- **£300 each** • **Rowan & Rowan**

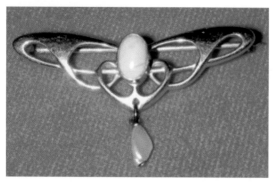

Locket and Collar ▼
- *1880*

Victorian silver locket on interlocking silver collar. Of Estruscan revival design, with 18ct gold ribbon inlay and etching to the silver of the locket.
- *length 23cm*
- **£450** • **Rowan & Rowan**

American Watch Bracelet ▼
- *1940*

Gold-plated American watch bracelet, similar to one worn by Gloria Swanson.
- **£250** • **Linda Bee**

Art Nouveau Brooch ◄
- *1900*

Art Nouveau 9ct gold brooch set with a turquoise and baroque pearl drop. Marked "Liberty & Co".
- *length 3cm*
- **£480** • **Gooday Gallery**

Marine Items

Cylindrical Rule ◄
- *1929*

A very rare cranberry-glass cylindrical rule with silver mounts.
- *length 30cm*
- £399   • Langfords Marine

Brass Candlestick Balance ▼
- *1840*

Victorian brass candlestick or lighthouse balance. The words, "POSTAL BALANCE" embossed with a spring scale on a circular moulded foot.
- *height 17cm*
- £299   • Langfords Marine

Oak Helm ▲
- *circa 1910*

A six-spar oak ship's wheel, bound in brass.
- £299   • Ocean Leisure

Taffrail Ship's Log ▲
- *circa 1920*

Polished and lacquered brass Cherub III. Outrigger pattern in original, specially constructed and weatherproofed box. By Thos. Walker and Son.
- £250   • Ocean Leisure

Pater Compass ▲
- *circa 1800*

Dry-card Pater compass on a two-inch turned wood base. Hand-painted card. By Stockert, Bavaria, for the English market.
- £429   • Ocean Leisure

Ship in a Bottle ▲
- *1900*

Three-masted ship in a bottle with coastal scene in the background.
- *length 30cm*
- £480   • Langfords Marine

Ship in a Bottle ►
- *1885*

Square-rigged ship in a bottle on a mahogany stand.
- *length 28cm*
- £320   • Langfords Marine

Silver & Pewter

Early Georgian Salts ▼
- *1744*

A pair of circular silver salts with gilt interiors made in London, raised on animal feet from mask decoration.
- *diameter 7cm*
- **£475**   ● Percy's Ltd

Napkin Ring ▼
- *1890*

Single triangular napkin ring, with engraved fern decoration and "Daisy" inscription. Birmingham.
- **£250**   ● Stephen Kalms

Ewer ▲
- *1860*

Kashmiri silver ewer with intricate floral designs with snake handle terminating in snake's head thumbpiece on lid.
- *height 29cm*
- **£350**   ● Namdar

Sovereign Case ◄
- *1912*

Heart-shaped silver sovereign case, engraved with floral designs. By E.J. Houlston, Birmingham.
- *length 5cm*
- **£250**   ● Linden & Co

Hand Mirror ▲
- *1892*

Silver hand mirror with swirl fluted back and twist fluted handle. Made in Birmingham.
- *length 29cm*
- **£350**   ● Linden & Co

Edwardian Card Box ▲
- *1900*

A silver card box profusely engraved with floral meanderings, including two original sets of cards from Vienna. Made in Birmingham.
- *height 6cm*
- **£475**   ● Stephen Kalms

Scallop-Shaped Dishes ►
- *1884*

A pair of Victorian silver dishes, naturalistically formed as scallop shells.
- *width 12cm*
- **£325**   ● Stephen Kalms

Assorted Pewter ▼
- **19th century**

Flagon, two chalices and two plates in English pewter. Quart capacity flagon banded with domed lid and moulded base.
- **£425**   • Castlegate

Georgian Charger ▼
- **circa 1750**

English George II charger, with single reeded rim in polished pewter, by Richard King.
- *diameter 42cm*
- **£275**   • Jane Stewart

Armenian Cross ➤
- **circa 1800**

A silver Armenian reliquary cross with a lozenge-shaped river pearl and coral stones.
- *height 30cm*
- **£350**   • Iconastas

Silver Goblet ▲
- **1874**

A single silver engraved goblet with gilded interior, a knop stem raised on a splayed base, made by Mappin and Webb of London.
- *height 13cm*
- **£300**   • Stephen Kalms

Mustard Pot ▼
- **1910**

Elegant George V drum mustard pot with pierced pattern and blue glass liner.
- *height 9cm*
- **£375**   • Linden & Co

Art Nouveau Tureen ▼
- **1900**

Art Nouveau pewter tureen on a splayed foot, with a finial top and twin handles.
- *9.5cm x 24cm*
- **£280**   • Gooday Gallery

Pewter Dish ▼
- **1905**

Art Nouveau pewter dish with three lobed sections decorated with an organic design of stylised leaves by Gallia.
- *20cm x 31cm*
- **£250**   • Gooday Gallery

Tudric Dish ◀
- **1895**

Art Nouveau by Liberty in polished pewter with hammered finish on a splayed pedestal foot, with organic, pierced handles.
- *diameter 32cm*
- **£250**   • Percy's

Sporting Items

Pond Yacht ➤
- *circa 1960*

Model gaff-rigged pond yacht on a brass stand.
- *height 98cm*
- £325 • Sean Arnold

Croquet Set ▲
- *1930*

Portable croquet set on mahogany stand with brass handle and feet, containing four mallets, hoops and red, black, yellow and blue balls.
- £495 • Sean Arnold

Signed Manchester United Shirt ▼
- *1999–2000*

Manchester United football shirt from the 2000 season. The shirt is signed by the team including key players such as Beckham, Giggs and Keane.
- £350 • Star Signings

Original Racquets ▼
- *circa 1880*

Original racquet for playing the game of racquets, with original stringing and leather press.
- *height 58cm*
- £475 • Sean Arnold

Barcelona Team Photograph ▼
- *1999–2000*

Photograph of the 1999–2000 Barcelona squad. Signed at Wembley stadium, in the match against Arsenal. Includes Rivaldo, Kluivert and Figo.
- £350 • Star Signings

Hazell Tennis Racquet ◀
- *1934*

Hazell streamlined tennis racquet of first aerodynamic design. Blue star, gut strings.
- *length 68cm*
- £425 • Sean Arnold

Brass Salmon Reel ▲
- *circa 1910*

Solid brass salmon fly fishing reel with bone handle and original leather case, by C. Farlow.
- *diameter 11cm*
- **£450**   • **Reel Thing**

Murdoch Rod ▲
- *circa 1920*

The Murdoch split-cane fishing rod made by Hardy.
- *length 395cm*
- **£295**   • **Reel Thing**

Hardy "St George" ▼
- *circa 1932*

Hardy "St George" $3\frac{1}{8}$ inch. Brass and metal components. Agate line guard.
- **£295**   • **Reel Thing**

Landing Net ▼
- *early 20th century*

Poker pattern, bamboo landing net. Bowed wood hoop and brass fittings.
- **£275**   • **Reel Thing**

Hardy Telescopic Gaff ◄
- *early 20th century*

Deep-sea telescopic gaff, for big game fishing. With belt clip. Brass with rosewood handle and spring safety clip.
- **£250**
- **Reel Thing**

Leather Fly Wallet ▲
- *circa 1900*

Hardy leather fly wallet with a good fly selection, and leather strap.
- *length 17cm*
- **£275**   • **Reel Thing**

Hunter's Display Case ▲
- *circa 1923*

Display case showing tusks and moths of India.
- *32cm x 30cm*
- **£420**   • **Holland & Holland**

Duck Decoy ▲
- *circa 1890*

Vintage duck decoy. Painted in natural colourings.
- **£295**   • **Reel Thing**

Tools

Austrian Sideaxe ◄
- *circa 1820*

An early 19th-century Austrian sideaxe, cast in iron with a beechwood haft, used for forestry and related occupations.
- *length 65cm*
- **£475** • The Old Tool Chest

Dividers ▲
- *circa 17th century*

Large pair of English dividers for transferring measurements to substantial items of furniture.
- *length 62cm*
- **£280** • The Old Tool Chest

Jointer Plane ▼
- *circa 1890*

A French jointer plane of exceptional length; all wood with original cutter bar.
- *length 103cm*
- **£475** • The Old Tool Chest

Oak Router ▲
- *circa 1760*

Oak router with rosewood wedge, carved in the form of three turrets with beautiful patina.
- *width 17.5cm*
- **£480** • Tool Shop Auctions

Badger Plane ▼
- *circa 1790*

Large wooden "badger" plane, for planing into corners by John Green, a famous tool-maker of the late 18th/early 19th century.
- *length 33cm*
- **£250** • The Old Tool Chest

Plumb Board and Bob ▲
- *1830*

George IV decorative mahogany plumb board and bronze plumb bob in classical style with simple carved ornamentation.
- *width 45cm*
- **£470** • Tool Shop Auctions

Expert Tips

Saw blades, chisels and braces, if rusty or corroded, can be improved by the application of light oil, and then rubbed down with an emery cloth. Early spirit levels were often made of rare woods; if carefully restored, they can be very attractive.

Sash Fillister ▲
- *1870*

Rare Victorian beautifully crafted sash fillister in solid Brazilian rosewood with brass fittings and boxwood stem wedges.
- *length 25cm*
- **£400** • Tool Shop Auctions

Victorian Level ▼
- *1860*

Victorian rare waisted rosewood and brass level.
- **£445** • Tool Shop Auctions

Toys, Games & Dolls

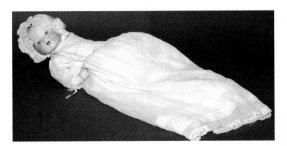

Shirley Temple Doll ▲
- *circa 1930s*
Very collectable Shirley Temple composition doll, with all original clothes and club badge.
- *height 65cm*
- £450   • Dolly Land

Hubert the Cottage Youth ▲
- *1812*
"Hubert the cottage youth" by S.& J. Fuller. Comprises a head, one hat and six colour pictures showing Hubert in various scenes from his life. With original slip case.
- *height 13cm*
- £400   • Judith Lassalle

Catterfelda Doll ▼
- *circa 1870*
A German hand-painted porcelain doll made by Catterfelda, wearing the original lace dress.
- *height 66cm*
- £480   • Dolly Land

Dutch Rocking Horse ▼
- *circa 1900*
Dutch wooden rocking horse with two semi-circular side panels. All originally painted and with horsehair tail.
- *height 63cm*
- £425   • R. Conquest

Dream Baby ◀
- *1920*
Dream Baby doll in excellent condition with open-and-close eyes, original white apparel and painted features.
- *length 34cm*
- £325   • Big Baby Little Baby

Replica Bear ▲
- *1991*
A replica of a Steiff 35PB teddy bear of 1904, with string mechanism and sealing wax nose.
- *height 50cm*
- £450   • Dolly Land

Steiff Bear ▲
- *circa 1991*
A Steiff bear, one of a limited edition of 300 which were made only for the UK market in 1991. This is a replica of a Steiff bear salvaged from the *Titanic* and sold for £94,400.
- *height 48cm*
- £450   • Dolly Land

Racing Car ◄
- **1930**
Clockwork metal, blue and red French racing car with driver, by Charles Rossignol, Paris.
- *length 40cm*
- **£485** • **Lennox Gallery**

Ford Sedan ▲
- **1950s**
Marusan Ford Sedan toy car. A lovely bright yellow with lithographed seat and crosshatched floor. Chrome bumper, lights and trim.
- *length 25.5cm*
- **£250** • **Pete McAskie**

Acrobat on Trapeze ▼
- **1880**
French somersaulting acrobat on trapeze wearing blue conical hat and red tunic with painted face. Made from wood and paper.
- *height 23cm*
- **£350** • **Judith Lassalle**

Roly Poly ▲
- *circa 1860–1870*
Roly Poly papier mâché with weighted balance in the figure of a large boy wearing tunic of blue and red with yellow buttons.
- *height 14cm*
- **£350** • **Judith Lassalle**

Selection of Marbles ▲
- *late 19th century*
Selection of marbles on solitaire board. Most are onion skins of various colours. The marbles alone are extremely collectable.
- **£300** • **Judith Lassalle**

Expert Tips

The first toy trains were made in the 1830s, of either metal or wood.

Royal Scot Train ➤
- **1935**
Red English Royal Scot metal train with black trim and wheels.
- *length 26cm*
- **£425** • **Jeff Williams**

Hornby Nord Loco ◄
- *circa 1930*
Hornby Nord Loco and Tender. Clockwork mechanism. Brown tin plate and black Hornby front.
- *length 43cm including tender*
- **£295** • **Wheels of Steel**

Wine-Related Items

Grape Hod ▼
- *1890*

Grape-harvesting container with leather straps for carrying with the Saint-Emilion Château Gironde emblem.
- *height 65cm*
- £420   • R. Conquest

Leather Vessel ▼
- *circa 1800*

Small leather hand-cut and stretched drinking vessel.
- *height 18cm*
- £250   • Holland & Holland

Silver-Plated Fruit Press ▲
- *19th century*

A fruit press by Kirby & Beard & Co. With beaten organic-shaped stem and maker's name plaque.
- *height 32cm*
- £440   • Lesley Bragge

Wine Labels ▲
- *circa 1900*

A late-Victorian set of six wine labels, enamelled by Thomas Goode & Co, South Audley Street, London, and in their original velvet-lined case with leather exterior.
- £385   • Lesley Bragge

French Wine Taster ▼
- *circa 1880*

Parisian silver wine taster with circular body with domed centre, with embossed design.
- *diameter 5cm*
- £350   • Linden & Co.

French Corkscrew ▼
- *circa 1890*

A French L'Excelsior patent corkscrew with ivory handle.
- *height 18cm*
- £250   • Emerson

Lady's Legs Corkscrew ◄
- *circa 1894*

A German, folding corkscrew with enamelled lady's legs which open to form the crossbar.
- *height 6.5cm*
- £310   • Emerson

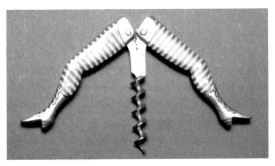

There follows a list of antique dealers, many of whom have provided items in the main body of the book and all of whom will be happy to assist within their areas of expertise.

No.1 Castlegate Antiques
(ref: Castlegate)
1-3 Castlegate, Newark, Notts NG24 1AZ
Tel: 01636 701877
18th and 19th-century furniture and decorative objects.

Abacus Antiques
(ref: Abacus)
Grays Antiques Market,
58 Davies Street, London W1Y 2LP
Tel: 020 7629 9681
Antiques.

A. D. Antiques
The Swan at Tetsworth, High Street,
Tetsworth, Thame,
Oxfordshire, OX9 7AB
Tel: 07939 508171
www.adantiques.com
Decorative arts.

After Noah
121 Upper Street, London N1 1QP
Tel: 020 7359 4281   Fax: 020 7359 4281
and
261 King's Rd, London SW3 5EL
Tel: 020 7351 2610   Fax: same
Specializes in oak and similar furniture, iron and brass beds, decorative items, candlesticks, mirrors, lighting, kitchenalia and jewellery. Furnishment and furbishment.

Albany Antiques
(ref: Albany)
8-10 London Road, Hindhead,
Surrey GU26 6AF
Tel: 01428 605528   Fax: 01428 605528
Georgian furniture, glass, china and works of art.

AM-PM
V35 Antiquarius Antiques Market,
135 King's Rd, London SW3
Tel: 020 7351 5654
Antique and modern watches.

Antique Warehouse
9-14 Dentford Broadway, London SE8 4PA
Tel: 020 8691 3062   Fax: 020 8469 0295
martyn@antiquewarehouse.co.uk
www.antiquewarehouse.co.uk
Decorative antiques.

Sean Arnold Sporting Antiques
(ref: Sean Arnold)
1 Pembridge Villas, London W2 4XE
Tel: 020 7221 2267   Fax: 020 7221 5464
Sporting antiques.

Ash Rare Books
(ref: Ash Books)
153 Fenchurch St, London EC3M 6BB
Tel: 020 7626 2665   Fax: same
www.ashrare.com
Books, maps and prints

Garry Atkins
107 Kensington Church St, London W8 7LN
Tel: 020 7727 8737   Fax: 020 7792 9010
English and continental pottery to 18th century, small furniture to 19th century.

Aurum
Grays Antiques Market,
58 Davies Street,
London W1K 5LP
Tel: 020 7409 0215
www.aurum.uk.com
Antique and period jewellery, and Shelly china.

Dr Colin B. Baddiel
B24 Grays Antiques Market,
Davies Mews,
London W1
Tel: 020 7408 1239
Fax: 020 74939344
Die-cast and tin toys.

Barham Antiques
(ref: Barham)
83 Portobello Road, London W11 2QB
Tel: 020 7727 3845   Fax: 020 7727 3845
Victorian walnut and inlaid continental furniture, writing boxes, tea caddies, inkwells and inkstands, glass epergnes, silver plate, clocks, paintings.

Linda Bee
Grays in the Mews Antiques Market, 1-7 Davies
Mews, London W1Y 1AR
Tel: 020 7629 5921   Fax: 020 7629 5921
Mobile: 0956 276384
Vintage costume jewellery and fashion accessories.

Julia Bennett
Tel: 01279 850279
Mobile: 0831 198 550   Mobile: 0831 614009
Period furniture and decorative antiques.

Beverley
30 Church Street, London NW8 8EP
Tel: 020 7262 1576   Fax: 020 7262 1576
Art Nouveau, Art Deco, decorative objects.

Big Baby & Little Baby Antiques
(ref: Big Baby Little Baby)
Grays Antiques Market, Davies Mews, London W1
Tel: 020 8367 2441   Fax: 020 8366 5811
Dolls, teddies, prams and related collectables.

Bizarre
24 Church Street, London NW8 8EP
Tel: 020 7724 1305   Fax: 020 7724 1316
www.antiques-uk/bizarre
Decorative art 1900-1950, Art Deco.

Paolo Bonino
Stand S001, Alfie's Antique Market,
13–25 Church Street,
London NW8 8DT
Tel: 020 7723 6066
European twentieth-century glass and ceramics.

Book & Comic Exchange
14 Pembridge Road, London W11
Tel: 020 7229 8420
www.buy-sell-trade.co.uk
Also pop memorabilia.

Malcolm Bord Gold Coin Exchange
(ref: Malcolm Bord)
16 Charing Cross Road, London WC2H 0HR
Tel: 020 7836 0631 / 240 0479   Fax: 020 7240 1920
Dealing in all types of coins, medals and bank notes.

Lesley Bragge
(ref: Bragge)
Fairfield House, High Street,
Petworth, West Sussex
Tel: 01798 342324
Wine-related items.

F. E. A. Briggs Ltd
77 Ledbury Road, London W11 2AG
Tel: 020 7727 0909
Marine items.

S. Brunswick
13 Church Street, London NW8 8DT
Tel: 020 7724 9097   Fax: 020 8902 5656
House, garden and conservatory.

Butchoff Interiors
(ref: Butchoff Interiors)
229 Westbourne Grove, London W11 2SE
Tel: 020 7221 8163   Fax: 020 7792 8923
www.butchoff.co.uk
adam@butchoff.co.uk
Furniture, lighting.

C.A.R.S of Brighton
(ref: CARS)
4-4a Chapel Terrace Mews, Kemp Town,
Brighton BN2 1HU
Tel: 01273 622 722   Tel/Fax: 01273 601 960
cars@kemptown-brighton.freeserve.co.uk
www.carsofbrighton.co.uk
*Classic automobilia & regalia specialists, children's
pedal cars.*

Jasmin Cameron
Antiquarius Antiques Market,
135 King's Rd, London SW3 4PW
Tel: 020 7351 4154   Fax: 020 7351 4154
Mobile: 0374 871257
*Specialising in drinking glasses and decanters 1750-
1910, vintage fountain pens, writing materials and
Rene Lalique glass/Art Deco.*

Vivienne Carroll
Antiquarius, Stand N1,
135 King's Road, London SW3 4PW
Tel: 020 7352 8882   Fax: 020 7352 8734
Silver, jewellery, porcelain and ivory.

Mia Cartwright Antiques
(re: Mia Cartwright)
20th C. Theatre Arcade,
291 Westbourne Grove, London W11
Tel: 01273 579700   Mobile: 0956 440260
Saturdays only.

Circa
L43, Grays Mews Antiques Market,
1- 7 Davies Mews, London W1Y 2LP
Tel: 01279 466260   Fax: 01279 466260
Mobile: 07887 778499
Decorative and collectable glass.

John Clay Antiques
(ref: John Clay)
263 New King's Road, London SW6 4RB
Tel: 020 77315677
claycorps@yahoo.com
*Furniture, objets d'art, silver and clocks, 18th- and
19th-century.*

Teresa Clayton (TRIO)
(ref: Trio)
L24, Grays Mews Antiques Market,
1-7 Davies Mews, London W1Y 2LP
Tel: 020 7493 2736   Fax: 020 7493 9344
Perfume bottles and Bohemian glass.

Clock Workshop, The
(ref: Clock Workshop)
17 Prospect St, Caversham, Reading RG4 8JB
Tel: 0118 947 0741
Fine clocks for decoration.

Garrick D. Coleman
(ref: G.D. Coleman)
75 Portobello Rd, London W11 2QB
Tel: 020 7937 5524   Fax: 020 7937 5530
coleman_antiques_london@compuserve.com
Antiques, fine chess sets and glass paperweights.

Marc Constantini Antiques
(ref: M. Constantini)
313 Lillie Road, London SW6 7LL
English.

Rosemary Conquest
4 Charlton Place, London N1 8AJ
Tel: 020 7359 0616
*French, Dutch and English lighting, furniture and
decorative objects.*

Hilary Conqy
K6, Antiquarius Antiques Market, 135 King's Rd,
London SW3 4PW
Tel: 020 7352 2099
Jewellery.

**Curios Gardens & Interiors
(ref: Curios)**
130c Junction Road, Archway, London N19
Tel: 020 7272 5603
*Decorative objects especially unusual items; general
antiques, pictures and garden furniture.*

Decodence
21 The Mall, Camden Passage, 359 Upper St,
London N1 0PD
Tel: 020 7354 4473   Fax: 020 7689 0680
gad@decodence.demon.co.uk
Classic plastics and vintage radios.

Dodo
Stand Fo73, Alfie's Antiques Market,
13-25 Church Street, London NW8 8DT
Tel: 020 7706 1545   Fax: 0207 724 0999
Posters, tins and advertising signs 1890-1940.

Dolly Land
864 Green Lanes, Winchmore Hill,
London N21 2RS
Tel: 020 8360 1053   Fax: 020 8364 1370
www.dollyland.com
Dolls, teddies, trains, die-cast limited editions.

**Drummonds Architectural Antiques Ltd
(ref: Drummonds)**
Kirkpatrick Buildings, 25 London Road (A3),
Hindhead, Surrey GU26 6AB
Tel: 01428 609444   Fax: 01428 609445
www.drummonds/arch.co.uk
*Period bathrooms, period flooring, brassware,
furniture, garden statuary and period gates.*

**Emerson Antiques
(ref: Emerson)**
Shop 2, Bourbon & Hanby Antiques Centre
Shop, 151 Sydney St, London SW3 6NT
Tel: 020 7351 1807   Fax: 020 7351 1807
iemerson @aol.com
Corkscrews and collectables.

**Finchley Fine Art Gallery
(ref: Finchley)**
983 High Road, North Finchley, London N12 8QR
Tel: 020 8446 4848
finchleyfineart@ukonline.uk
*Watercolours and paintings, fine 18th- and 19th-
century furniture, pottery, porcelain and smalls.*

**Jack First
(ref: J. First)**
Grays Mews Antiques Market, 1-7 Davies Mews,
London W1Y 2LP
Tel: 020 7409 2722
Silver and pewter.

David Ford
2 Queenstown Road, Battersea, London SW8
Tel: 020 7622 7547
forddesign@compuserve.com
*An eclectic range of furniture, furnishings and
accessories.*

Ford Design
2 Queenstown Road, Battersea, London SW8
Tel: 020 7622 7547

A.& E. Foster
Little Heysham, Forge Rd,
Naphill, Bucks HP14 4SU
Tel: 01494 562024   Fax: 01494 562024
*Early treen, European works of art.Strictly by
appointment only.*

Nicholas Fowle Antiques
Websdales Court, Bedford Street, Norwich,
Norfolk NR2 1AR
Tel: 01603 219964   Fax: 01603 219964
*17th-, 18th- and 19th-century furniture; works of
art; valuations.*

**Lynda Franklin Antiques
(ref: L. Franklin)**
25 Charnham Street, Hungerford, Berkshire
RG17 0EJ
Tel: 01488 682404   Fax: 01488 686089
Mobile: 0831 200834
*Antiques and interior design, French furniture -
17th- and 18th-century.*

**Fulham Antiques
(ref: Fulham)**
318-320 Munster Road, London SW6 6BH
Tel: 020 7610 3644   Fax: 020 7610 3644
aeantique@tesco.net
*Furniture, restoration of lacquer, gilding and
French polish.*

Ghaznavid
A30 Grays Antiques Market,
1–7 Davies Mews,
London W1Y 2LP
Tel: 020 7629 2813
Fax: 020 8896 2114

Roman. 3338

**Gordon's Medals Ltd
(ref: Gordon's Medals)**
Grays Mews Antique Market,
1-7 Davies Mews, London W1Y 2LP
Tel: 020 7495 0900
Medals.

Gosh
39 Great Russell Street, London, WC1B 3PH
Tel: 020 7436 5053   Fax: 020 7436 5053
Comics.

Solveig Gray, Anita Gray
(ref: Anita Gray)
Grays Mews Antiques Market, 1-7 Davies Street,
London W1Y 2LP
Tel: 020 74081638   Fax: 020 74950707
info@chinese-porcelain.com
Antique Oriental works of art.

Great Grooms Antique Centre
(ref: Great Grooms)
Great Grooms, Parbrook,
Billinghurst, West Sussex RH14 9EU
Tel: 01403 786202
Fax: 01403 786224
www.great-grooms.co.uk
*Furniture, porcelain, jewellery, silver, glass and
pictures.*

Henry Gregory
82 Portobello Rd, London W11 2QD
Tel: 020 7792 9221
Antique jewellery, silver and objects.

Gütlin Clocks and Antiques
(ref: Gütlin Clocks)
616 King's Rd, London SW6
Tel: 020 7384 2439   Fax: 020 7384 2439
www.gutlin.com
mark@gutlin.com
*Longcase clocks, mantel clocks, furniture and
lighting, all 18th- and 19th-century.*

Robert Hales Antiques
(ref: Robert Hales)
131 Kensington Church St, London W8 7LP
Tel: 020 7229 3887   Fax: 020 7229 3887
Fine Oriental arms and armour, tribal art.

Adrian Harrington
64A Kensington Church St, London W8 4DB
Tel: 020 79371465   Fax: 020 73680912
www.harringtonbooks.co.uk
rarerare@harringtonbooks.co.uk

Henry Hay
(ref: H. Hay)
Unit 5054, 2nd Floor, Alfie's Market,
13/25 Church Street, London NW8
Tel: 020 7723 2548
*Art Deco, chrome and brass lamps, bakelite
telephones, 20th-century.*

Holland & Holland
31-33 Bruton St, London W1X 8JS
Tel: 020 7499 4411   Fax: 020 7409 3283
Guns.

Jonathan Horne
(ref: J. Horne)
66b & 66c Kensington Church St,
London W8 4BY
Tel: 020 7221 5658   Fax: 020 7792 3090
Early English pottery, needlework and works of art.

Howard & L. Hamilton
(ref: Howard & Hamilton)
151 Sydney Street, London SW3 6NT
Tel: 020 7352 0909   Fax: 020 7352 0066
Scientific instruments.

Christopher Howe Antiques
(ref: Howe)
93 Pimlico Road, London SW1W 8PH
Tel: 020 7730 7987   Fax: 020 7730 0157
c.howe@easynet.co.uk
*Furniture and lighting from the 17th- to 20th-
century.*

Huxtable's Old Advertising
(ref: Huxtable's)
Alfie's Market, 13-25 Church Street,
London NW8 8DT
Tel: 020 7724 2200   Mobile: 01727 833445
*Advertising, collectables, tins, signs, bottles,
commemoratives, old packaging from late Victorian.*

Hygra, Sign of the
(ref: Hygra)
2 Middleton Road, London E8 4BL
Tel: 020 7254 7074   Fax: 0870 125 669
www.hygra.com
boxes@hygra.com

Iconastas
5 Piccadilly Arcade, London SW1
Tel: 020 7629 1433   Fax: 020 7408 2015
Russian fine art.

J.A.N. Fine Art
134 Kensington Church St, London W8 4BH
Tel: 020 7792 0736   Fax: 020 7221 1380
*Specialising in Oriental porcelain, painting and works
of art.*

Japanese Gallery Ltd
(ref: Japanese Gallery)
66d Kensington Church Street,
London W8 4BY
Tel: 020 7729 2934
Fax: 020 7229 2934

*Japanese woodcut prints, Japanese ceramics, swords,
armour and Japanese dolls.*

P.L. James
590 Fulham Road, London SW6 5NT
Tel: 020 7736 0183
*Gilded mirrors, English and Oriental lacquer, period
objects and furniture.*

Jessop Classic Photographica
67 Great Russell Street, London WC1
Tel: 020 7831 3640 Fax: 020 7831 3956
classic@jessops.co.uk
Classic photographic equipment, cameras and optical toys.

Stephen Kalms
Chancery House, 53-64 Chancery Lane,
London WC2 1QS
Tel: 020 7430 1254 Fax: 020 7405 6206
Mobile: 0831 604001
stephen@skalms.freeserve.co.uk
Fine silver specialist.

Kenworthy's Ltd
226 Stamford Street, Ashton-under-Lyne,
Manchester OL6 7LW
Tel: 0161-330 3043
Jewellery, bijouterie and snuff boxes; silver and old Sheffield plate; valuations.

Kitchen Bygones
13–15 Church Street,
Marylebone,
London NW8 8DT
Tel: 020 7258 3405
Fax: 020 7724 0999
Kitchenalia.

Lacquer Chest, The
(ref: Lacquer Chest)
75 Kensington Church St, London W8 4BG
Tel: 020 7937 1306 Tel: 020 7938 2070
Fax: 020 7376 0223
Country antiques.

Langfords
(ref: Langfords)
Vault 8/10, London Silver Vaults,
Chancery Lane, London WC2A 1QS
Tel: 020 7242 5506 Fax: 020 7405 0431
vault@langfords.com
www.langfords.com
Antique and modern silver and silver plate.

Langfords Marine Antiques
(ref: Langfords Marine)
The Plaza, 535 King's Rd, London SW10 0SZ
Tel: 020 7351 4881 Fax: 020 7352 0763
Marine antiques – ship models and nautical items.

Judith Lassalle
7 Pierrepont Arcade, Camden Passage,
London N1 8EF
Tel: 020 7607 7121
Optical toys, books and games.

Linden & Co (Antiques) Ltd
Vault 7, London Silver Vaults,
Chancery Lane, London WC2A 1QS
Tel: 020 7242 4863 Fax:020 7405 9946
Silver, plate, works of art.

London Antique Gallery
66e Kensington Church St, London W8 4BY
Tel: 020 7229 2934 Fax: 020 7229 2934
pomolondon@hotmail.com
Porcelain including Dresden, Meissen, English and Sevres; French and German bisque dolls.

Stephen Long Antiques
348 Fulham Road, London SW10 9UH
Tel: 020 7352 8226
English Pottery, 18th- and 19th-century, English painted furniture, toys and games, household and kitchen items, chintz, materials and patchwork.

Mac's Cameras
262 King Street, Hammersmith, London W6 0SJ
Tel: 020 8846 9853
Antique camera equipment.

Pete McAskie Toys
(ref: Pete McAskie)
A12/13, Grays Mews Antiques Market,
1-7 Davies St, London W1Y 2LP
Tel: 020 7629 2813 Fax: 020 7493 9344
Tin toys – 1880-1980.

Magpies
152 Wandsworth Bridge Rd, London SW6 2UH
Tel: 020 7736 3738
Antique collectables and lighting, door furniture and kitchenalia.

A. P. Mathews
283 Westbourne Grove, London W11
Tel: 01622 812590
Antique luggage.

More Than Music Collectables
(ref: More Than Music)
C24/25, Grays Mews Antiques Market,
1-7 Davies Mews, London W1Y 2LP
Tel: 020 7629 7703 Fax: 01519 565 510
www.mtmglobal.com
morethnmus@aol.com
Rock and pop music memorabilia, specialising in The Beatles.

Motor Books
(ref: Motor)
33 St Martin's Court, London, WC2N 4AN
Tel: 020 7836 3800 Fax: 020 7497 2539
Motoring books.

Mousa Antiques
(ref: Mousa)
B20, Grays Mews Antiques Market,
1-7 Davies Mews, London W1Y 1AR
Tel: 020 7499 8273 Fax: 020 7629 2526
Bohemian glass specialists.

Music & Video Exchange
(ref: Music & Video)
38 Notting Hill Gate, London W11 3HX
Tel: 020 7243 8574
www.mveshops.co.uk
CDs, tapes, vinyl – deletions and rarities.

Myriad Antiques
(ref: Myriad)
131 Portland Rd, London W11 4LW
Tel: 020 7229 1709
Decorative objects and furniture for the house and garden.

Stephen Naegel
Grays Mews Antiques Market, 1/7 Davies Mews,
London W1Y 2LP
Tel: 020 7491 3066   Fax: 01737 845147
www.btinternet.com/~naegel
Toys.

Namdar Antiques
(ref: Namdar)
B22, Grays Mews Antiques Market,
1-7 Davies Mews, London W1Y 2LP
Tel: 020 7629 1183   Fax: 020 7493 9344
Metalware, Oriental and Islamic ceramics, glassware and silver.

Colin Narbeth & Son Ltd
(ref: C. Narbeth)
20 Cecil Court, London WC2N 4HE
Tel: 020 7379 6975   Mobile: 01727 811244
Colin.Narbeth@btinternet.com
www.colin-narbeth.com
Scripophily.

North West Eight
(ref: NW8/North West 8)
36 Church Street, London NW8 8EP
Tel: 020 7723 9337
Decorative antiques.

Edward Nowell & Sons
12 Market Place, Wells, Somerset BA5 2RB
Tel: 01749 672415   Tel: 01749 678738
Fax: 01749 673519
Mid 18th-century English furniture; Chinese blue and white porcelain; silver and jewellery; valuations.

Ocean Leisure
11-14 Northumberland Avenue,
London WC2N 5AQ
Tel: 020 7930 5050   Fax: 020 7930 3032
www.oceanleisure.co.uk
info@oceanleisure.co.uk

Old Father Time Clock Centre
1st floor, 101 Portobello Rd, London W11 2QB
Tel: 020 8546 6299   Fax: 020 8546 6299
Mobile: 0836 712088
www.oldfathertime.netclocks@oldfathertime.net
Unusual and quirky clocks.

Telephone Co, The
(ref: Old Telephone Co)
The Battlesbridge Antiques Centre,
The Old Granary, Battlesbridge,
Essex SS11 7RE
Tel: 01245 400 601
www.theoldtelephone.co.uk
Antique and collectable telephones.

Old School
130c Junction Road,
Tufnell Park,
London N19
Tel: 020 7272 5603
Gardens and interiors.

Old Tool Chest, The
(ref: Old Tool Chest)
41 Cross Street, Islington, London N1 2BB
Tel: 020 7359 9313
Tools for all trades – ancient and modern.

Jacqueline Oosthuizen
23 Cale St, Chelsea Green, London SW3 3QR
Tel: 020 7352 6071   Mobile: 0385 258 806
Staffordshire figures, jewellery, decorative ceramics.

Pieter Oosthuizen
(ref: P. Oosthuizen)
Unit 4, Bourbon Hanby Antiques Centre,
151 Sydney St, London SW3
Tel: 020 7460 3078   Fax: 020 7376 3852
Dutch and European art nouveau pottery and Boer War memorabilia.

Oriental Rug Gallery
(ref: Oriental)
230 Upper High Street,
Guildford, Surrey GU1 3JD
Tel: 01753 623000   Fax: same
www.orientalruggallery.com
rugs@orientalruggallery.com
Russian, Afghan, Turkish and Persian carpets, rugs and kelims; Oriental objets d'art.

Paul Orssich
2 St Stephen's Terrace, London SW8 1DH
Tel: 020 7787 0030   Tel: 020 7735 9612
paulo@orssich.com
www.orssich.com
Old books and maps.

Pars Antiques
(ref: Pars)
A14/15, Grays Mews Antique Market,
1-7 Davies Mews, London W1Y 1AR
Tel: 020 7491 9889   Fax: 020 7493 9344
Mobile: 0410 492552
Antiquities.

Percy's Silver Ltd
(ref: Percy's)
Vault 16, The London Silver Vaults,
Chancery Lane, London WC2A 1QA
Tel: 020 7242 3618 Fax: 020 7831 6541
www.percys-silver.com
sales@percys-silver.com
Antique silver.

Photographer's Gallery, The
(ref: Photographer's Gallery)
5 Great Newport Street, London WC2H 7HY
Tel: 020 7831 1772 Fax: 020 7836 9704
info@photonet.org.uk
www.photonet.org.uk

David Pickup Antiques
(ref: David Pickup)
115 High Street, Burford,
Oxfordshire OX18 4RG
Tel: 01993 822555 Mobile: 0860 469959
Fine English furniture and works of art.

Radio Days
87 Lower Marsh, London SE1 7AB
Tel: 020 7928 0800 Fax: 020 7928 0800
*1930s-70s' lighting, telephones, radio, clothing
and magazines.*

Rainbow Antiques
(ref: Rainbow)
329 Lillie Road, London SW6 7NR
Tel: 020 7385 1323 Mobile: 0870 0521693
Mobile: 07775 848494
fabio@rainbow-antiques.demon.co.uk

Ranby Hall Antiques
(ref: Ranby Hall)
Barnby Moor, Retford, Nottingham DN22 8JQ
Tel: 01777 860696 Fax: 01777 701317
www.ranbyhall.antiques-gb.com
paul.wyatt4@virgin.net
*Antiques, decorative items and contemporary
objects.*

Mark Ransom Ltd
(ref: Mark Ransom)
62&105 Pimlico Road, London SW1W 8LS
Tel: 020 7259 0220 Fax: 020 7259 0323
contact@markransom.co.uk
Decorative Empire/French furniture.

Gordon Reece Gallery
(ref: Gordon Reece)
16 Clifford Street, London, W1X 1RG
Tel: 020 7439 0007 Fax: 020 7437 5715
and
24 Finkle Street, Knaresborough,
North Yorks HG5 8AA
Tel: 01423 866219 Fax: 01423 868165
www.gordonreecegalleries.com
*Flat woven rugs and nomadic carpets, tribal
sculpture, jewellery, furniture, decorative and
non-European folk art, especially ethnic and
Oriental ceramics.*

Reel Poster Gallery, The
(ref: Reel Poster Gallery)
72 Westbourne Grove, London W2 5SH
Tel: 020 7727 4488 Fax: 020 7727 7799
www.reelposter.comellen@reelposter.com
Posters.

Reel Thing, The
(ref: Reel Thing)
17 Royal Opera Arcade,
Pal Mall, London SW1Y 4UY
Tel: 020 7976 1830 Fax: 020 7976 1850
www.reelthing.co.uk
reelthinginfo@reelthing.co.uk
Purveyors of vintage sporting memorabilia.

Retro Exchange
(ref: Retro)
20 Pembridge Road, London W11
Tel: 020 7221 2055 Fax: 020 7727 4185
www.i/fel.trade.co.uk
Space age style furniture, 50s' kitsch.

Riverbank
The High Street, Petworth,
West Sussex GU28 0AU
Tel: 01798 344401 Fax: 01798 343135
antiques@riverbank-antiques.com
Antiques and the picturesque.

Michele Rowan
(ref: Rowan & Rowan)
V36, Antiquarius Antiques Market,
135 King's Rd, London SW3 4PW
Tel: 020 7352 8744 Fax: 020 7352 8744
rowan&rowan@aol.com
Antique jewellery.

Russell Rare Books, T.A.
Cherrington Rare Books Ltd
(ref: Russell Rare Books)
81 Grosvenor St, London W1X 9DE
Tel: 020 7629 0532 or 020 7493 1343
Fax: 020 7499 2983
folios.co.uk
Rare books.

C.F. Seidler
Unit 4, Bourbon Hanby Antiques Centre,
151 Sydney Street, London SW3
Tel: 020 7460 3078
*Dutch and European Art Nouveau pottery and Boer
War memorabilia.*

Shahdad Antiques
(ref: Shadad/Shahdad)
A16/17, Grays Mews Antiques Market,
1-7 Davies Mews, London W1Y 2LP
Tel: 020 7499 0572 Fax: 020 7629 2176
amir@arts1.freeserve.co.uk
Islamic and ancient works of art.

Bernard Shapero
2 Saint George St, London W1R 0EA
Tel: 020 7493 0876   Fax: 020 7229 7860
rarebooks@shapero.com
www.shapero.com
Rare books.

Sharif
27 Chepstow Corner, London W2 4XE
Tel: 020 7792 1861   Fax: 020 7792 1861
Oriental rugs, kilims, textiles and furniture.

Shiraz Antiques
(ref: Shiraz)
H 10/11, Grays Mews Antiques Market,
1-7 Davies Mews, London W1Y 2LP
Tel: 020 7495 0635
Islamic and ancient works of art.

Sinai Antiques
(ref: Sinai)
219-21 Kensington Church St, London W8 7LX
Tel: 020 7229 6190   Fax: 020 7221 0543
Antiques and works of art.

Ian Spencer
(ref: Ian Spencer, Spencer)
17 Godfrey Street, London SW3 3TA
Mobile: 0973 375940
Large desks, sets of chairs and dining tables.

Star Signings
Unit A18/A19, Grays Mews Antiques Market,
1-7 Davies Mews, London W1Y 2LP
Tel: 020 7491 1010   Fax: 020 7491 1070
starsignings@hotmail.com
Sporting autographs and memorabilia.

Jane Stewart
C 26/27, Grays Mews Antiques Market,
Davies Mews, London W1Y 2LP
Tel: 020 7355 333
*Pewter early 17th- to 19th-century, oak,
writing slopes.*

Constance Stobo
31 Holland St, London W8 4NA
Tel: 020 79376282
*English lustreware, Staffordshire animals, Wemyss,
18th- and 19th-century pottery.*

June & Tony Stone
(ref: J. & T. Stone)
75 Portobello Rd, London W11 2QB
Tel: 020 7221 1121   Tel: 01273 500024
Mobile: 07768 382424
info@boxes.co.uk
Fine antique boxes.

Sugar Antiques
(ref: Sugar)
8-9, Pierrepont Arcade, Camden Passage,
London N1 8EF
Tel: 020 7354 9896   Fax: 020 8931 5642
Mobile: 0973 179 980
elayne@sugar-antiques.demon.co.uk
www.sugar-antiques.demon.co.uk
*Jewellery and costume jewellery, antique watches,
classic fountain pens.*

Mark Sullivan
(ref: M. Sullivan)
14 Cecil Court, London WC2N 4EZ
Tel: 020 7836 7056   Tel: 020 8741 7360
Fax: 020 8287 8492
Antiques and decoratives.

Stuart Talbot FRAS
(ref: Talbot)
65 Portobello Road, London W11 2QB
Tel: 020 8969 7011
Fine scientific instruments.

Swan at Tetsworth, The
(ref: The Swan)
High Street, Tetsworth, Thame,
Oxfordshire OX9 7AB
Tel: 01844 281777
Fax: 01844 281770
www.theswan.co.uk
Seventy dealers in historic Elizabethan coaching inn.

Talking Machine
(ref: Talk Mach)
30 Watford Way, Hendon, London NW4 3AL
Tel: 020 8202 3473   Fax: 020 8202 3473
www.gramophones.ndirect.co.uk
*Mechanical music, gramophones phonographs,
vintage records.*

Telephone Lines Ltd
304 High Street, Cheltenham, Glos GL50 3JF
Tel: 01242 583699   Fax: 01242 690033
Telephones.

Themes and Variations
231 Westbourne Grove, London W11 2SE
Tel: 020 7727 5531   Fax: 020 7221 6378
go@themesandvariations.co.uk
Post-war design.

Thimble Society, The
(ref: Thimble Society)
Geoffrey van Arcade, 107 Portobello Road,
London W11 2QB
Tel: 020 7419 9562
*Thimbles, sewing items, snuff boxes and lady's
accessories.*

Tool Shop Auctions
78 High Street,
Needham Market,
Suffolk IP6 8AW
Tel: 01449 722992
www.uktoolshop.com

*Auctioneers and dealers of antique woodworking
tools and new Japanese, French and American tools.*

Tredantiques
77 Hill Barton Road, Whipton, Exeter EX1 3PW
Tel: 01392 447082   Fax: 01392 462200
Mobile: 07967 447082
Furniture.

trio
(ref: Trio)
Grays Mews Antiques Market, 1-7 Davies Mews,
London W1Y 2LP
Tel: 020 7493 2736   Fax: 020 7493 9344
Perfume bottles and Bohemian glass.

Trio Antiques
Antiquarius, 131-141 King's Road,
London SW3 4PW
Tel: 020 7352 8734
Country style antiques.

Wheels of Steel
B 10/11, Grays Mews Antiques Market,
1-7 Davies Mews, London W1Y 2LP
Tel: 020 8505 0450   Fax: 020 7629 2813
Trains, toys.

Whitford Fine Art
(ref: Whitford)
6 Duke Street, St. James's, London SW1Y 6BN
Tel: 020 7930 9332   Fax: 020 7930 5577
*Oil paintings and sculpture, late 19th-century to
20th-century; post-war abstract and pop art.*

Wilde Ones
283 King's Road, London SW3 5EW
Tel: 020 7352 9531   Fax: 020 7349 0828
shop@wildeones.com
Jewellery.

Jeff Williams
Grays Antiques Market,
58 Davies Street,
London W1K 5LP
Tel: 020 7629 7034
Toy trains.

Youlls Antiques
(ref: Youlls)
28 Charnham Street, Berks,
Hungerford RG17 0EJ
Tel: 01488 682046   Fax: 01488 684335
www.youll.combruce.
youll@talk21.com
French and English furniture and decorative items.

Zaheim
52 Ledbury Road, Westbourne Grove,
London W11
Tel: 020 7629 1433   Mobile: 0585 930 630
Russian works of art.

Zoom
Arch 65, Cambridge Grove, Hammersmith,
London W6 0LD
Tel: 07000 966 620   Tel/Fax: 020 8846 9779
Mobile: 0958 372975
www.retrozoom.com
eddiesandham@hotmail.com
*1950s-1970s' furniture, lighting and unusual
retro objects.*

MEASUREMENT CONVERSION CHART

This chart provides a scale of measurements converted from centimetres and metres to feet and inches.

1cm	$\frac{2}{5}$in
2cm	$\frac{4}{5}$in
3cm	$1\frac{1}{10}$in
4cm	$1\frac{3}{5}$in
5cm	2in
10cm	$3\frac{7}{8}$in
15cm	$5\frac{9}{10}$in
20cm	$7\frac{3}{4}$in
25cm	$9\frac{4}{5}$in
30cm	$11\frac{4}{5}$in
40cm	1ft $3\frac{3}{4}$in
50cm	1ft $7\frac{2}{3}$in
75cm	2ft $5\frac{1}{2}$in
1 m	3ft $3\frac{1}{3}$in
1.25m	4ft $1\frac{1}{5}$in
1.5m	4ft 11in
1.75m	5ft $8\frac{9}{10}$in
2m	6ft $6\frac{3}{4}$in
2.25m	7ft $4\frac{3}{5}$in
2.5m	8ft $2\frac{2}{5}$in
3m	9ft $10\frac{1}{10}$in